DK

Rapping Up Chemistry

with Matt Green

THE RAPPING SCIENCE TEACHER

From the author:

To my incredible wife, Helen – there would be no science raps without you. Thank you for being my constant encourager, for believing in me from the very beginning, and for giving me that first push to step in front of the camera. You are, and always have been, my number one supporter.
Huge thanks to my mum and dad for instilling in me the value of education and shaping my path to becoming a teacher, and to my wonderful in-laws, Emma and Mike, for your unwavering support.
My heartfelt gratitude goes to my management, Wendy Woolfson Talent and PR, for creating this incredible publishing opportunity. Wendy and Hannah – your inspiring work and guidance turn my dreams into reality.
Finally, thank you to DK for believing in this project and bringing it to life.

Author Matt Green, The Rapping Science Teacher
Author Contributor John Kavanagh

Produced for DK by
Editorial Just Content Limited
Design Fourth Wall

Senior Editor Amelia Jones
Managing Editor Katherine Neep
Managing Art Editors Sarah Corcoran, Elizabeth Arnoux
Pre-Production Designer Rohit Singh
Senior Production Controller Meskerem Berhane
Publisher Sarah Forbes
Managing Director, Learning Hilary Fine

First published in Great Britain in 2026 by
Dorling Kindersley Limited
20 Vauxhall Bridge Road,
London SW1V 2SA

The authorised representative in the EEA is
Dorling Kindersley Verlag GmbH. Arnulfstr. 124,
80636 Munich, Germany

Lyrics copyright © Matt Green 2026
Matt Green has asserted his right to be identified as the author of the lyrics in this work
Text and design copyright © 2026 Dorling Kindersley Limited
A Penguin Random House Company
10 9 8 7 6 5 4 3 2 1
001–352645–Jan/2026

All rights reserved.
No part of this publication may be reproduced, stored in or introduced into a retrieval system, or transmitted, in any form, or by any means (electronic, mechanical, photocopying, recording, or otherwise), without the prior written permission of the copyright owner. DK values and supports copyright. Thank you for respecting intellectual property laws by not reproducing, scanning or distributing any part of this publication by any means without permission. By purchasing an authorised edition, you are supporting writers and artists and enabling DK to continue to publish books that inform and inspire readers. No part of this publication may be used or reproduced in any manner for the purpose of training artificial intelligence technologies or systems. In accordance with Article 4(3) of the DSM Directive 2019/790, DK expressly reserves this work from the text and data mining exception.

A CIP catalogue record for this book is available from the British Library.
ISBN: 978-0-2417-7155-6

Printed and bound in China

www.dk.com

This book was made with Forest Stewardship Council™ certified paper – one small step in DK's commitment to a sustainable future.
Learn more at www.dk.com/uk/information/sustainability

Welcome from Matt

Welcome to Rapping Up Chemistry – by me, Matt Green The Rapping Science Teacher!

This book takes everything I've learnt from all my years of teaching in schools and on social media and lays it out in an easy-to-use revision format.

Helping students to understand science means a huge amount to me, so I have put blood, sweat and tears into this guide to make Chemistry revision not just simple, but unforgettable.

First, read each topic section to understand the key ideas. Then move to the RAPPING UP! section to lock it in with a short, punchy rap that makes the facts stick.

Forget boring textbooks – this guide is your secret weapon, designed to help you master GCSE Chemistry and walk into your exams with total confidence.

Let's drop the beat and start learning.
Rap. Revise. Remember!

Contents

Atomic Structure and the Periodic Table — 5
- Atomic Structure 6
- Electronic Configuration 7
- Separation Techniques 8
- The Periodic Table 10
- Groups of the Periodic Table 12
- Brain Booster 14

Bonding, Structure and Properties of Matter — 15
- Ionic Bonding 16
- Ionic Structures 17
- Covalent Bonding 18
- Simple Molecules vs. Giant Covalent Structures 19
- Allotropes of Carbon 20
- Metals 22
- Brain Booster 24

Quantitative Chemistry — 25
- Formulae 26
- Equations 27
- Relative Masses 28
- Moles 29
- Chemical Calculations 30
- Brain Booster 32

Chemical Changes — 33
- The Reactivity Series 34
- Extraction of Metals 35
- Metals and Acids 36
- Neutralisation Reactions 37
- Acids and Titrations 38
- Electrolysis 40
- Brain Booster 42

Energy Changes — 43
- Exothermic and Endothermic Reactions 44
- Reaction Profiles 46
- Calculating Energy Changes 47
- Chemical Cells 48
- Fuel Cells 49
- Brain Booster 50

Rates of Reaction — 51
- Rates of Reaction 52
- Measuring Rates of Reaction 53
- Collision Theory 54
- Reversible Reactions 56
- Equilibrium 57
- Brain Booster 58

Organic Chemistry — 59
- Crude Oil and Hydrocarbons 60
- Fractional Distillation 62
- Cracking and Alkenes 64
- Reactions of Alkenes 66
- Alcohols 67
- Carboxylic Acids 68
- Esters 69
- Addition Polymers 70
- Condensation Polymers 71
- Natural Polymers 72
- DNA 73
- Brain Booster 74

Chemical Analysis — 75
- Pure Substances 76
- Formulations 77
- Identification of Common Gases 78
- Identification of Cations and Anions 80
- Instrumental Methods 82
- Brain Booster 84

Chemistry of the Atmosphere — 85
- The Early Atmosphere 86
- The Current Atmosphere 87
- Global Climate Change 88
- Air Pollution 90
- Brain Booster 92

Earth's Resources — 93
- Sustainable Development 94
- Potable Water 95
- Treating Waste Water 96
- Alternative Metal Extraction 98
- Ceramics 99
- Reduce, Reuse, Recycle 100
- Life Cycle Assessment 101
- Corrosion 102
- Preventing Corrosion 103
- Alloys 104
- Composites and Polymers 105
- The Haber Process 106
- Fertilisers 107
- Brain Booster 108

Answers 109
Exam Board References 111
Acknowledgments 112

Atomic Structure and the Periodic Table

At the end of this chapter, you should be able to:

- ✓ Label the subatomic particles in an atom.
- ✓ State the charges and relative masses of the three subatomic particles.
- ✓ Draw the electronic configuration of any of the first 20 elements when provided with a periodic table.
- ✓ Explain how mixtures are separated by crystallisation, distillation, filtration, fractional distillation and paper chromatography.
- ✓ Describe how elements are arranged in the modern periodic table.
- ✓ State where metals and non-metals are found in the periodic table.
- ✓ Describe the physical properties of the alkali metals (Group 1) and the halogens (Group 7).
- ✓ Explain why the noble gases (Group 0) are unreactive or inert.

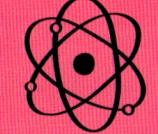

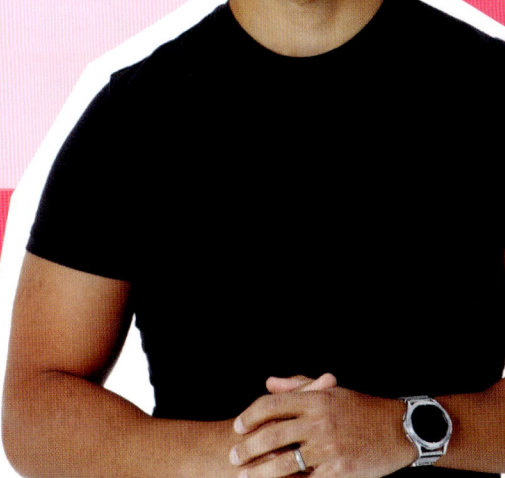

Atomic Structure and the Periodic Table

Atomic Structure

Key facts

- All substances are made of atoms.
- Elements are made of only one type of atom, whereas compounds are made of two or more different atoms bonded together.
- Atoms are made of protons, neutrons and electrons.
- Atoms can lose or gain electrons, forming charged particles known as ions.
- There are just over 100 different elements, which can all be found in the periodic table.

Science skills

Atomic number = number of protons

Mass number = number of protons and neutrons

To work out the number of neutrons in a particular atom, you need to find the difference between the mass number and the atomic number.

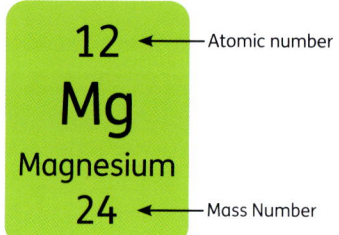

12 ← Atomic number
Mg
Magnesium
24 ← Mass Number

An **atom** is the smallest unit of matter, made up of **protons**, **neutrons** and **electrons**. The protons and neutrons are in the **nucleus**, while the electrons orbit in **shells** around the nucleus. Atoms are incredibly tiny, with a typical atom measuring around one ten-millionth of a millimetre. To give you an idea of how small that is, a single page in this book is approximately a million atoms thick.

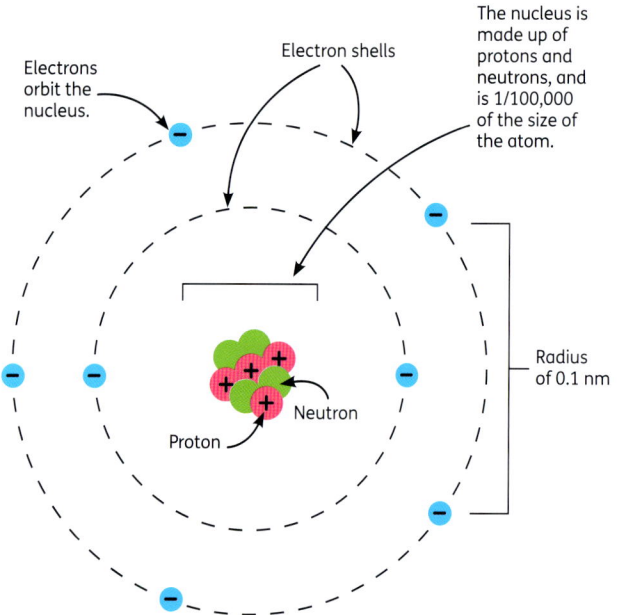

Electrons orbit the nucleus.
Electron shells
The nucleus is made up of protons and neutrons, and is 1/100,000 of the size of the atom.
Radius of 0.1 nm
Proton
Neutron

Atoms, ions and isotopes

When an atom gains or loses one or more electrons, it becomes an ion. Positively charged ions formed by the loss of electrons are called **cations**. Negatively charged ions formed by the gain of electrons are called **anions**. Isotopes are different versions of the same element. Isotopes have the same number of protons but different numbers of neutrons.

	Charge	Mass
⊕ Proton	+1	1
● Neutron	0	1
⊖ Electron	−1	0

Atomic Structure and the Periodic Table

Electronic Configuration

Key facts

- Electrons in an atom are arranged in shells or energy levels.
- The first shell (closest to the nucleus) has the lowest energy and can hold up to two electrons.
- The second and third shells can hold up to eight electrons each.
- There is a fourth shell, which can also hold electrons if needed.
- The number of electrons in the outermost shell determines the reactivity of the element.

Electronic configuration

Electronic **configuration** describes how electrons are arranged around the nucleus of an atom. The atom shown below is aluminium. It has 13 electrons. The first shell has two electrons, the second shell has eight electrons. Both these shells are full. The remaining three electrons go into the outer shell. The number of **outer shell electrons** indicates which group the element belongs to in the periodic table. In the case of aluminium, with three electrons in its outer shell, it is in Group 3. All elements in the same group react in a similar way as they all have the same number of electrons in the outer shell.

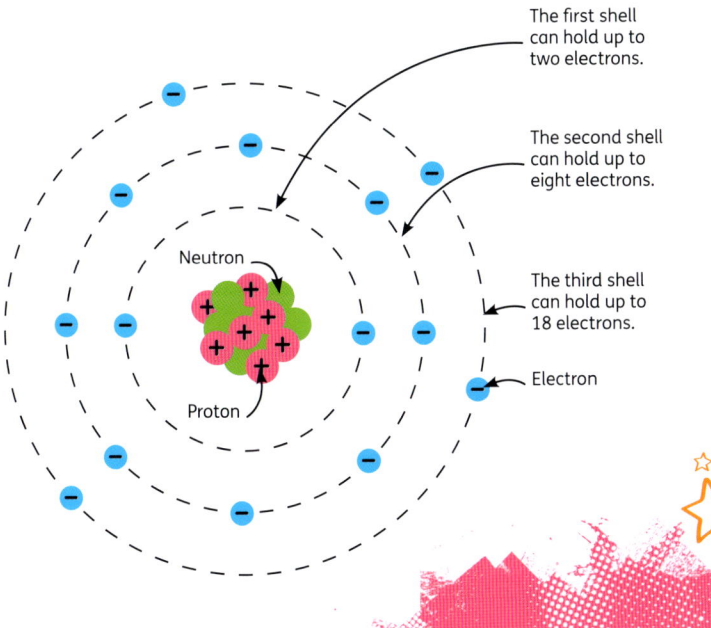

The first shell can hold up to two electrons.
The second shell can hold up to eight electrons.
The third shell can hold up to 18 electrons.
Electron
Neutron
Proton

RAPPING UP!

The **atom**? It's little.
That's usual. **Nucleus**?
The middle. That's usual.
Protons and **neutrons** – that's where they live.
Electrons are in shells, and they fill up like this:

Two up in the first
and in the next go eight.
If they're not completely full
they won't feel great.
In chemical reactions
they will lose or gain
an **electron** from that last shell
just to end that pain.

For an atom in **Group 1**
that really ain't that long.
All it's gotta do is
just lose one electron.
Now its charge will change
from zero to plus one.
It's no longer an atom;
you call it an ion.

Look now it's time for **Group 2**.
They become two plus;
it's two electrons they will lose.
The flip side is **Group 6 and 7**
they don't do the same;
to get a full shell it's electrons they will gain.

Group 7 atoms
they don't ever show kindness.
They don't give, they take
and then become one minus.
OIL RIG? I'll just leave you
with this famous saying:
it is oxidation is the loss,
reduction is the gain.

Atomic Structure and the Periodic Table

Separation Techniques

Key facts

- A mixture is a combination of two or more substances that are not chemically bonded together.
- Common mixtures include air, soil and sea water.
- Mixtures can be separated by physical processes such as crystallisation, distillation, filtration and paper chromatography.

Science skills

To calculate R_f values for a chromatogram you need to use the following equation:

$$R_f = \frac{\text{distance moved by substance}}{\text{distance moved by solvent}}$$

In the example chromatogram shown, the R_f value for red ink would be $4 \div 5 = 0.8$.

The baseline must be drawn in pencil so it does not run, and the solvent front needs to be established so that R_f values can be determined.

Mixtures can be separated through physical processes. As no chemical reactions occur during these processes, no new substances are created.

Chromatography

Chromatography is a technique used to separate mixtures in a solution. It works because the different substances have varying levels of **solubility** in a specific solvent. In chromatography, the **mobile phase** is the solvent that moves through the stationary phase. The **stationary phase** is the material (in the example shown, it is the chromatography paper), which does not move.

Filtration

Filtration is a method used to separate an **insoluble solid** from a liquid by passing the mixture through a **filter**.

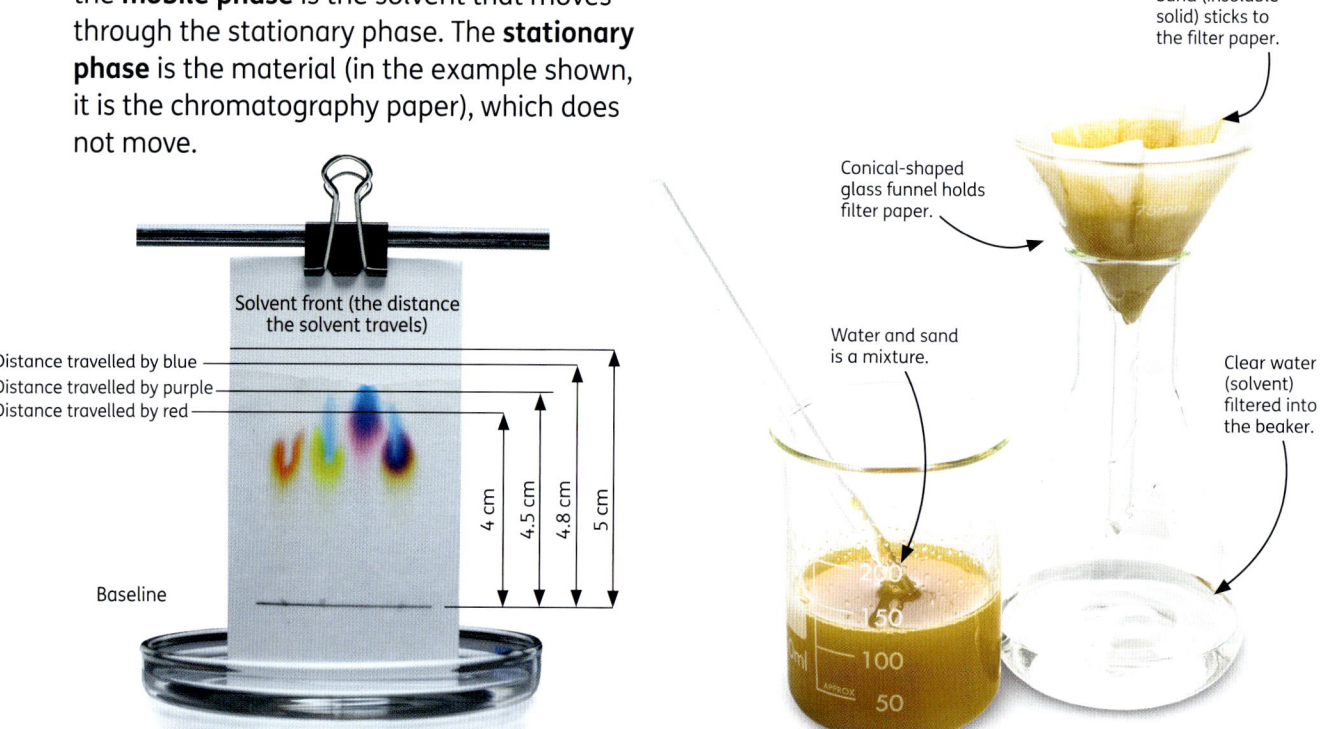

Atomic Structure and the Periodic Table

Crystallisation

Crystallisation is a process used to obtain a **pure solid** from its solution by **evaporating** the solvent.

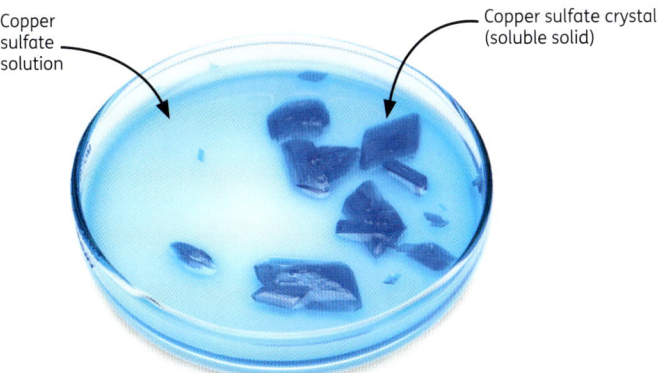

Copper sulfate solution

Copper sulfate crystal (soluble solid)

Fractional distillation

Fractional distillation is a laboratory technique used to separate a mixture of liquids with different boiling points by heating the mixture and condensing the components at various stages. You will revise this in more detail later on page 62.

Distillation

Distillation is a method used to separate a solvent from soluble solids dissolved in the solvent.

RAPPING UP!

They say this is a boring subject but I'm told my teaching's unique. Give me some **alcohol** and a **Bunsen**, here's a separation technique.

Rum is a mixture of these. Here is how you **separate**: water boils at 100 degrees, and for ethanol, 78.

Heat the mixture up for this stage. The ethanol finds it offensive. Watch it **evaporate**. In this tube right here, it condenses.

That was simple **distillation**, liquid separation depicted. Now if we look at filtration, that separates solids from liquids.

If the solid can dissolve that means we can't use filtration. There's another method we can involve: **evaporation** and **crystallisation**.

1. The mixture of water and ink in a flask is heated by a Bunsen burner.
2. Hot water vapour rises through the tube and cools.
3. Cool water is pumped around a Liebig condenser tube to help the hot water vapour cool and condense.
4. Pure, clear water runs down the tube and collects in the beaker.

Water has a lower boiling point than the ink, so it boils and evaporates into vapour.

Cool water vapour condenses in the tube.

Water out — Water in

Atomic Structure and the Periodic Table

The Periodic Table

Key facts

- The periodic table is a table containing all of the known elements, ordered by their atomic number (proton number).
- Elements are arranged into periods (horizontal rows) and groups (vertical columns) based on shared characteristics.
- Metals, found on the left and centre of the table, are typically shiny, good conductors of heat and electricity, malleable and ductile.
- Non-metals, found on the right-hand side of the periodic table, are often dull, poor conductors of heat and electricity, and brittle.
- The periodic table was first created by Dmitri Mendeleev in 1869; he arranged the elements by atomic mass and predicted the discovery of new elements.
- Mendeleev left gaps in his table that predicted the existence of elements that were discovered later.
- The modern periodic table is now arranged by atomic number.

For any student studying chemistry, the **periodic table** is an indispensable tool that provides a wealth of information. By organising elements by their **atomic number** and grouping them according to similar chemical properties, the periodic table can help you to predict how elements will react with one another, as well as identifying **trends in reactivity**.

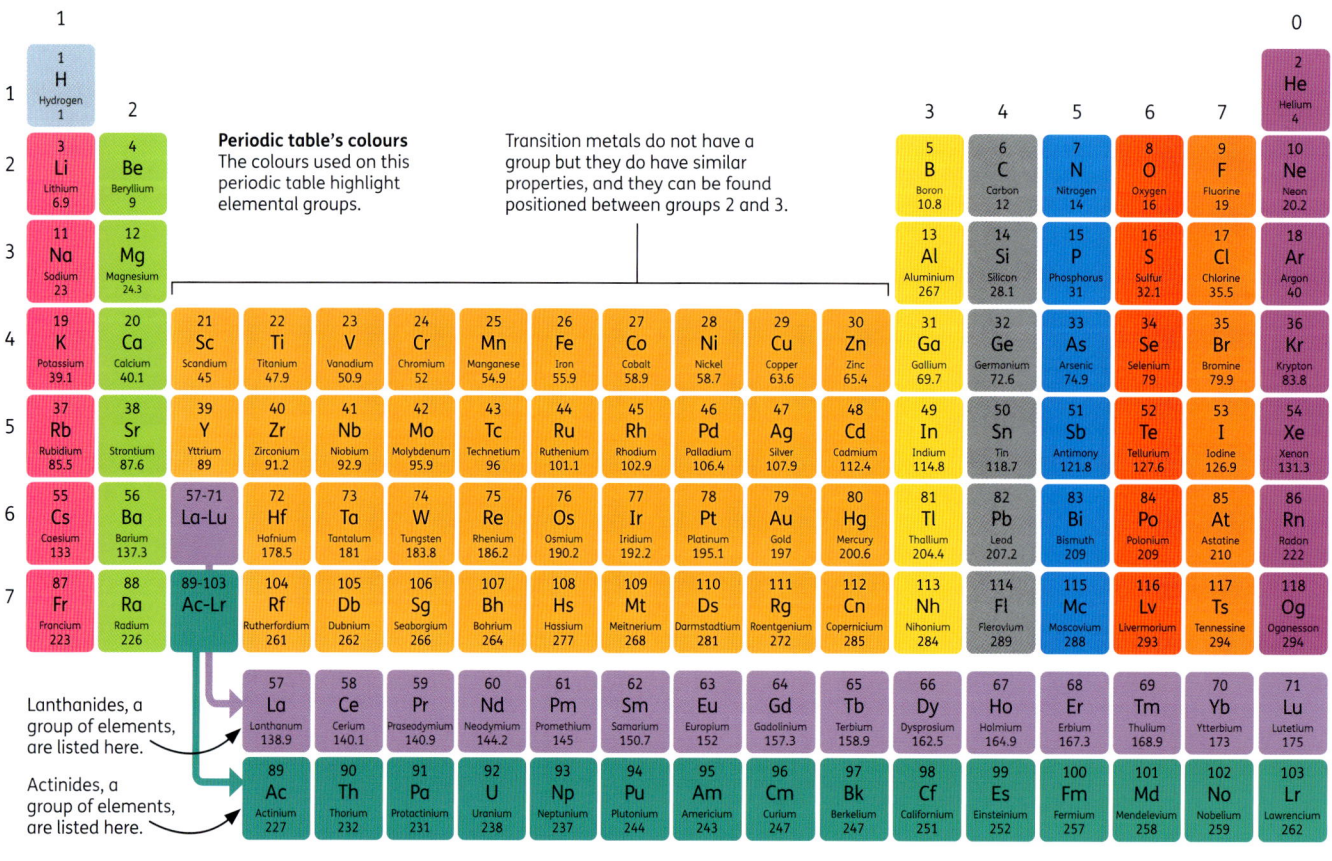

Atomic Structure and the Periodic Table

Science skills

Each element in the periodic table features additional pieces of information.

3 Li Lithium 6.9	
3	The atomic number
Li	The element's symbol
Lithium	The element's full name
6.9	The relative atomic mass

- the atomic number = number of protons
- the element's symbol = one or two letter shorthand code, unique for each element
- the relative atomic mass = the average mass of an element's atoms, including isotopes

The periodic table

The periodic table arranges all 118 known elements by their atomic number and similar chemical properties. Elements in the same group have similar chemical properties due to having the same number of electrons in their outer electron shell. About three-quarters of the elements are metals, while the remaining quarter are non-metals. Elements in the same row have the same number of electron shells. Elements in the same column have the same number of outermost electrons.

History of the periodic table

The periodic table was first introduced by Dmitri Mendeleev in 1869. Mendeleev arranged the known elements by their atomic mass and left gaps for elements that had yet to be discovered, predicting their properties with remarkable accuracy. Before Mendeleev, John Newlands made significant contributions with his "Law of Octaves" in 1864, proposing that every eighth element had similar properties when elements were ordered by atomic mass. This early attempt at classification highlighted periodic trends, although it was not widely accepted at the time.

RAPPING UP!

Looking at the periodic table
John Newland had to do what he was able.
In 1864, only a few **elements** known
atomic weight order was the way
that they were shown.

However, they noticed patterns.
Recurring properties with **atoms** is what happened.
Using atomic weight, it weren't the right way.
You can see some **elements** in the wrong place.

Move over John, we need someone new.
Dimitri Mendeleev - the man we turned to.
What this man did, wow you have to love it.
He left gaps here for elements
that weren't discovered.

He basically predicted properties of new elements.
Without him we'd never have had
this further development.
The tables new layout is hotter than Summer.
And elements are placed by **atomic number**.

Groups of the Periodic Table

Key facts

- The elements in Group 1 are known as the alkali metals and are highly reactive.
- The elements in Group 7 are called the halogens; they are very reactive non-metals.
- The elements in Group 0 are the noble gases; they are known for their lack of reactivity.
- The transition metals are in the middle block of the periodic table.

Exam tip

Group 1 elements become more reactive and their melting and boiling points decrease as you go down the group. Conversely, in Group 7, reactivity increases and melting and boiling points decrease as you move up the group.

Group 1

Group 1 elements, or **alkali metals**, form oxides and hydroxides that dissolve in water to form alkaline solutions. They are reactive and this reactivity increases going down the group. Like other metals, the alkali metals are good conductors of heat and electricity. However, they also have some unusual properties for metals:

- They have low melting and boiling points.
- They are soft enough to cut with a knife.
- They have a low density, with the first three floating on water.

Group 7

Group 7 elements, also known as the **halogens**, are highly reactive non-metals. They have relatively low melting and boiling points, which increase steadily down the group. All the halogens have distinct colours and are poor conductors of heat and electricity. Halogens are brittle in their solid form. They possess characteristically strong odours, can cause burns upon contact with skin, and are poisonous.

Pure lithium becomes dull when exposed to air. Pure sodium is a light silver colour. Pure potassium is a light silver colour. Pure rubidium is a dark silver colour. Pure caesium is a silver-gold colour.

Fluorine

Pure fluorine gas is pale yellow.

Chlorine

Pure chlorine gas is yellow–green.

Bromine

Pure bromine gas is red–brown.

Iodine

Pure iodine crystals are dark purple and shiny.

Atomic Structure and the Periodic Table

Group 0

Group 0 elements, also known as **noble gases**, are colourless, odourless gases with very low boiling points. Their atoms have full outer shells, making them unreactive. They are usually found as single atoms (monatomic). On page 16, you will find more about how atoms lose, gain or share electrons to achieve this stable electronic configuration. It is possible to see colours emitted by the noble gases if an electric current is passed through them.

Helium — Pure helium glows purple when electrified.

Neon — Pure neon glows orange when electrified.

Argon — Pure argon glows pale purple when electrified.

Krypton — Pure krypton glows blue-white when electrified.

Xenon — Pure xenon glows blue when electrified.

Radon — Pure radon is a transparent gas.

Transition metals

Transition metals, located in the centre of the periodic table, possess typical metallic properties and can form multiple ions. They are widely used as catalysts in the chemical industry due to their efficiency in speeding up reactions. These metals often create colourful **ionic compounds** that dissolve in water. Tight stoppers are fitted onto the flask so air does not react with the solution.

Titanium solutions are usually colourless unless combined with certain anions.

Chromium (Cr^{3+}) is a pale green colour.

This nickel ion is a pale turquoise colour.

Copper ions in a water solution are usually a pale sky blue colour.

14 Brain Booster

Atomic Structure and the Periodic Table Recap Quiz

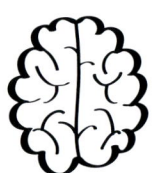

 Find a pen and paper and work through these revision questions. You will need access to a periodic table for some of the questions.

1. What is the atomic number of an element?
2. State the three subatomic particles and their charges.
3. Describe the structure of an atom.
4. Draw the electrons in shells found in an atom of sodium.
5. Describe how ions are formed.
6. State how elements are arranged in the periodic table.
7. Explain why noble gases are unreactive.
8. How can you separate a mixture of sand and water?
9. Use the periodic table on page 10 to determine the number of outer shell electrons in phosphorus.
10. Compare the properties of metals and non-metals.
11. Explain why noble gases are used in lighting applications.
12. Calculate the number of neutrons in an atom of carbon.
13. Explain why elements in the same group of the periodic table have similar chemical properties.

Check your answers on page **109**.

Bonding, Structure and Properties of Matter

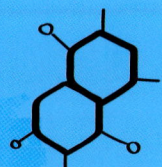

At the end of this chapter, you should be able to:

- ✓ State simple definitions for ionic, covalent and metallic bonding.
- ✓ Recall electronic configuration from the previous chapter and use it to determine bonding in a given substance.
- ✓ Explain how bonds are formed.
- ✓ Recall the link between bonding and noble gas electronic configuration.
- ✓ Describe some typical properties of ionic compounds.
- ✓ Describe why some covalently bonded substances can be simple molecules or giant structures.
- ✓ Describe some typical properties of covalent compounds.
- ✓ Describe the structures and properties of diamond, fullerenes, graphene and graphite.
- ✓ Explain how bonding affects some typical properties of metals, like electrical conductivity and malleability.
- ✓ Explain how the structure and bonding of a substance is linked to its physical properties.

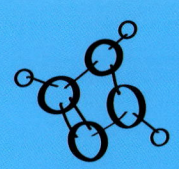

Bonding, Structure and Properties of Matter

Ionic Bonding

Key facts

- Ionic bonds form between metals and non-metals.
- Atoms gain or lose electrons during chemical reactions to achieve a stable full outer shell.
- Metals lose electrons to become positive ions (cations).
- Non-metals gain electrons to become negative ions (anions).
- Ionic compounds consist of alternating positive and negative ions.
- Ions are held by strong electrostatic attractions making a structure known as a giant ionic lattice.

This is I-ON-IC
It's a special kind of **bond**.

This is I-ON-IC
See this metals **electron**?

This is I-ON-IC
It transfers to a **non-metal**.

This is I-ON-IC
Now both outer shells are full.

In **ionic bonding** its all about shells.
When they're not completely full
they won't feel well.
In ionic bonding they will lose or gain
an electron from that last shell
just to end that pain.

Bonding

Atoms bond together to achieve a noble gas electronic configuration. Put more simply, atoms bond to obtain a full outer shell of electrons. When metals and non-metals react, they form **ionic bonds** by gaining or losing electrons. The other two types of bonding, **covalent bonding** (see pages 18 and 19) and **metallic bonding** (see pages 22 and 23), will be looked at later.

Forming an ionic bond

When metals and non-metals react, they form ionic bonds through **electrostatic attractions** between positive and negative charges. Metal atoms lose negatively charged electrons to become positively charged ions, while non-metal atoms gain those electrons to become negatively charged ions. The resulting ions have a stable, full outer shell of electrons.

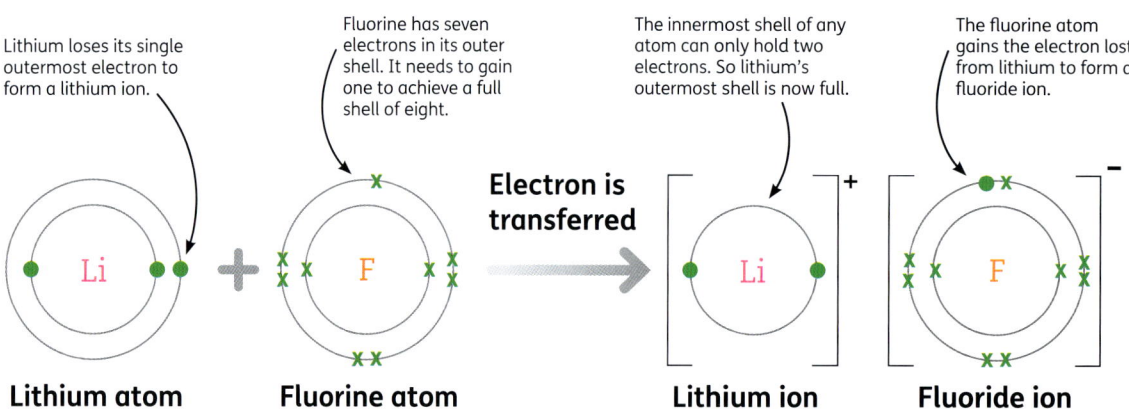

Lithium loses its single outermost electron to form a lithium ion.

Fluorine has seven electrons in its outer shell. It needs to gain one to achieve a full shell of eight.

The innermost shell of any atom can only hold two electrons. So lithium's outermost shell is now full.

The fluorine atom gains the electron lost from lithium to form a fluoride ion.

Electron is transferred

Lithium atom — Fluorine atom — Lithium ion — Fluoride ion

Bonding, Structure and Properties of Matter

In group 1 that really ain't that long.
All an atom does is just lose one electron.
Its charge change from zero to plus one.
It's no longer an atom, you call it an **ion**.

Look now it's time for group 2.
They become two plus it's two electrons they will lose.
The flip side is non-metals they don't do the same.
To get a full shell its electrons they will gain.

Non-metal atoms don't ever show kindness.
They don't give they take and then become minus.
OIL RIG? I'll just leave you with this famous saying.
It is **oxidation** is the loss, reduction is the gain.

Ionic Structures

Ionic compounds form when metals react with non-metals. These compounds consist of repeating three-dimensional networks of positive and negative ions and are held together by strong electrostatic forces. This systematic arrangement results in a stable giant ionic lattice.

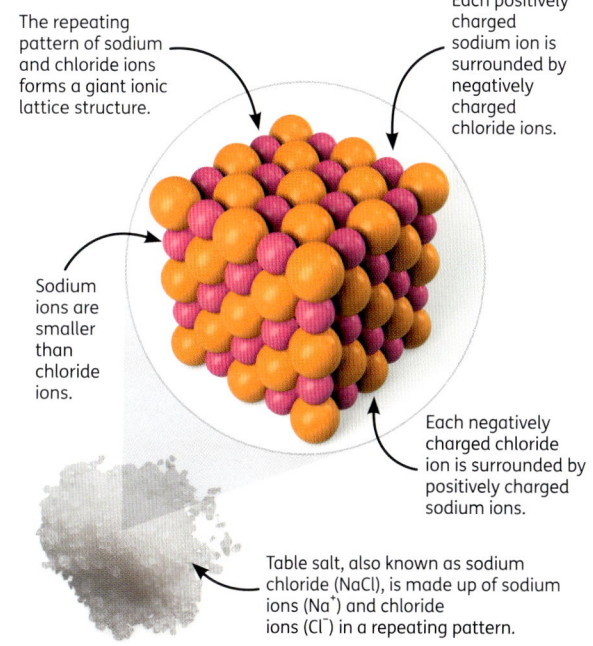

The repeating pattern of sodium and chloride ions forms a giant ionic lattice structure.

Each positively charged sodium ion is surrounded by negatively charged chloride ions.

Sodium ions are smaller than chloride ions.

Each negatively charged chloride ion is surrounded by positively charged sodium ions.

Table salt, also known as sodium chloride (NaCl), is made up of sodium ions (Na^+) and chloride ions (Cl^-) in a repeating pattern.

Properties of ionic compounds

Ionic compounds have distinct properties because of their ionic lattice structure. Solid ionic compounds are **crystalline** and usually have high melting and boiling points, though there are exceptions. In ionic solids, the ions are unable to move. When ionic compounds melt or dissolve, the ions separate and can move to carry an electrical charge. Some ionic compounds dissolve readily in water, while others do not. Sodium ions and chloride ions are arranged in a regular, repeating pattern in sodium chloride crystals.

Sodium chloride is a solid at room temperature.

Sodium ions (Na^+)

Chloride ions (Cl^-)

There are strong electrostatic attractions between the positive and negative ions.

Covalent Bonding

Key facts

- Covalent bonds occur between non-metal atoms.
- Covalent bonds are formed when two atoms share a pair of electrons so that each atom obtains a full outer shell.
- Only the electrons in the outermost shell are involved in this sharing.
- A shared pair of electrons between atoms is a covalent bond.

RAPPING UP!

This is a **covalent bond** between non-metal atoms. Each one needs an electron to have a full outer shell.

Right here imma show you one: overlap and then we're on. Draw an **X** and **O** to know where each one's from. Now count the full outer shells.

X O X O X O X O
That's how we draw out electrons.

X O X O X O X O
That's how we draw out electrons.

X O X O X O X O
That's how we draw out electrons.

Draw an **X** and **O** to know where each one's from. Now count the full outer shells.

Forming a covalent bond

The most stable electronic configuration for an atom is to have a full outer shell of electrons. By sharing electrons, each atom effectively gains one or more electrons to "fill" its outer shell and achieve the same stable electronic configuration as its nearest noble gas (see pages 10 and 11). Covalent bonds can form between non-metal atoms, which may be the same, such as in the **element** chlorine (Cl_2), or different, such as in the **compounds** water (H_2O) and carbon dioxide (CO_2).

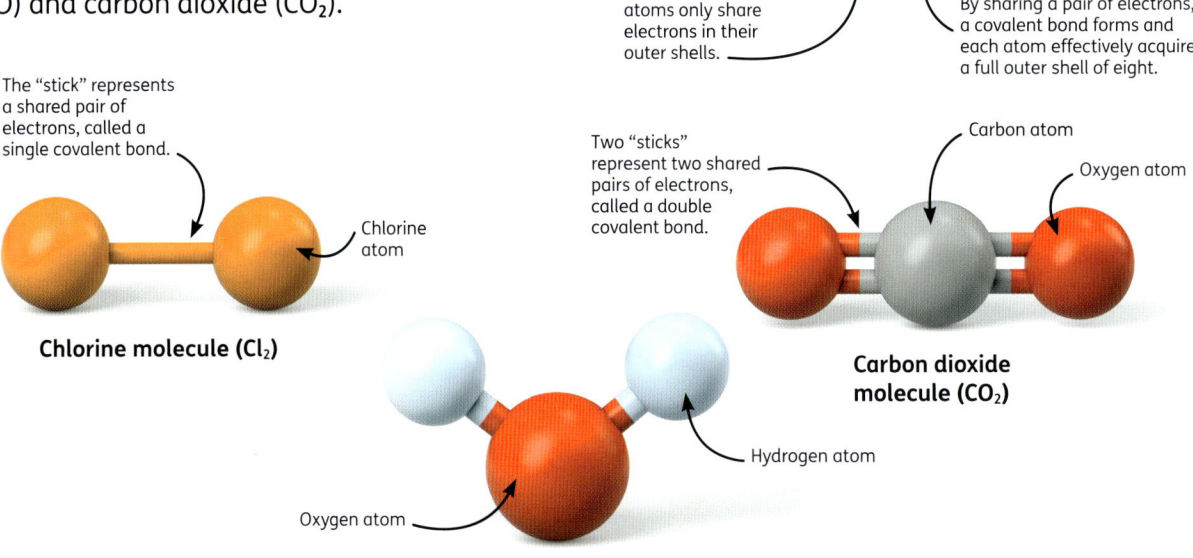

Each chlorine atom has seven electrons in its outer shell.

Electrons are represented by dots or crosses.

Covalent bonding diagrams often only show outer shell electrons as atoms only share electrons in their outer shells.

By sharing a pair of electrons, a covalent bond forms and each atom effectively acquires a full outer shell of eight.

The "stick" represents a shared pair of electrons, called a single covalent bond.

Chlorine atom

Chlorine molecule (Cl_2)

Two "sticks" represent two shared pairs of electrons, called a double covalent bond.

Carbon atom

Oxygen atom

Carbon dioxide molecule (CO_2)

Hydrogen atom

Oxygen atom

Water molecule (H_2O)

Simple Molecules vs. Giant Covalent Structures

It is possible for covalent bonding to produce small molecules or giant structures depending on the atoms involved. Giant covalent structures are covered in the section on diamond and graphite (see page 20). A simple molecule is made up of two or more non-metal atoms joined by one or more covalent bonds.

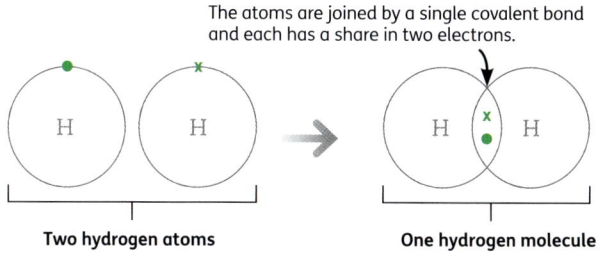

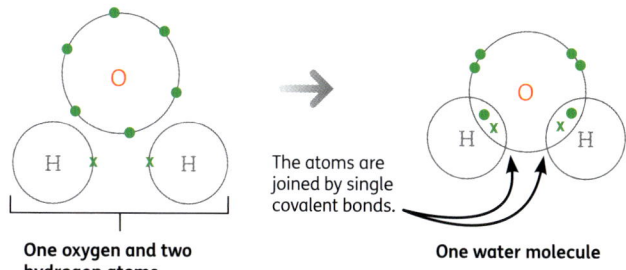

Properties of simple molecules

Simple molecular substances consist of atoms held by strong covalent bonds with weak intermolecular forces. These substances are usually gases or liquids at room temperature. Examples include water (H_2O) and chlorine (Cl_2), which have low melting and boiling points due to the minimal energy required to break their intermolecular forces.

Intermolecular forces

When simple molecular substances undergo melting or boiling, it is the intermolecular forces between the molecules that are disrupted, not the covalent bonds within the molecules. The larger the molecule, the greater the intermolecular forces between them, resulting in higher melting and boiling points.

Polymers

Polymers are large molecules (sometimes called macromolecules) formed by joining many small molecules together into long chains. The small molecules are called monomers. The monomers can be different or they can be all the same type of molecule. Most polymers are held together with covalent bonds. Polymers can be natural but they can also be artificial, such as plastics. Polymers are covered in the section on Organic Chemistry on page 59.

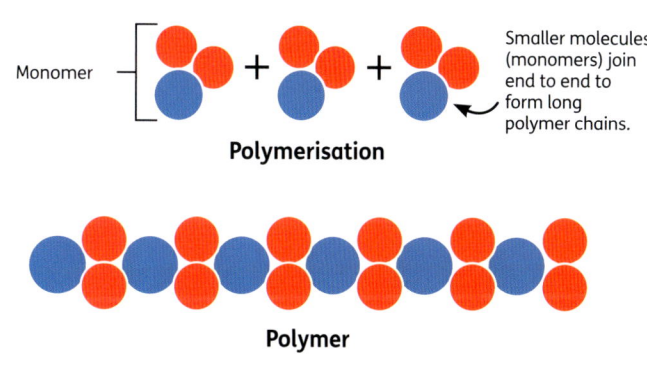

Bonding, Structure and Properties of Matter

Allotropes of Carbon

Giant covalent structures are formed by non-metal atoms in a repetitive giant lattice, creating very strong materials due to covalent bonding.

Key facts

- Giant covalent structures consist of numerous non-metal atoms bonded covalently, forming a repeating 3D lattice.
- Most giant covalent structures have high melting points, are hard and do not conduct electricity.
- Allotropes are different forms of an element.
- Diamond, graphite and graphene are allotropes of carbon, and are giant structures.
- Fullerenes are also allotropes of carbon but are classified as large carbon molecules.

Diamond

Each carbon atom in **diamond** is covalently bonded to four other carbon atoms. Diamond is known for its hardness. It does not conduct electricity, but it is an effective conductor of heat.

Diamond is the hardest naturally occurring substance.

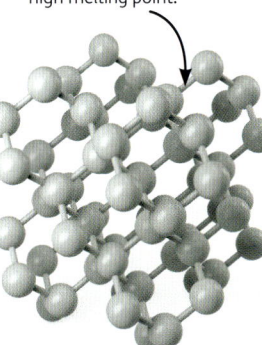

It takes a lot of energy to break all the covalent bonds in diamond, so it has a very high melting point.

Graphite

Each carbon atom in **graphite** is covalently bonded to three other carbon atoms, leaving one electron free. Graphite is softer than diamond but does conduct electricity because of the free delocalised electrons.

The carbon atoms in graphite form layers of hexagons.

The covalent bonds cannot be broken easily, so graphite has a high melting point.

Layers can slide over each other as the attraction between them is weak.

Graphene

Graphene is a single layer of graphite, known for its strength, low weight and ability to enhance other materials. It excels in conducting electricity.

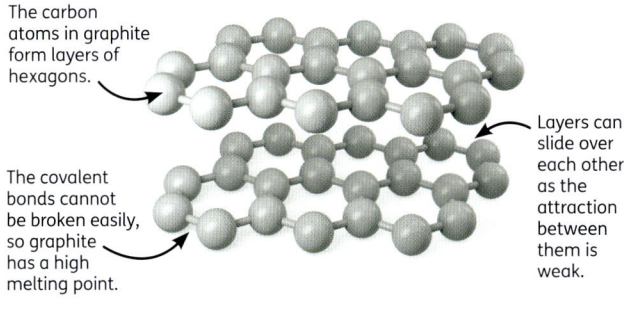

Graphene is almost transparent and very light.

The carbon atoms in graphene are arranged in hexagons.

Fullerenes

Fullerenes are another allotrope of carbon, consisting of large molecules shaped like balls or tubes. The first fullerene discovered was **buckminsterfullerene** (C_{60}), which is the most abundant of the fullerenes.

Buckyballs

In buckminsterfullerene, 60 carbon atoms are arranged in hexagons and pentagons, forming a spherical shape. Fullerenes are also able to encapsulate other atoms or molecules inside their structure.

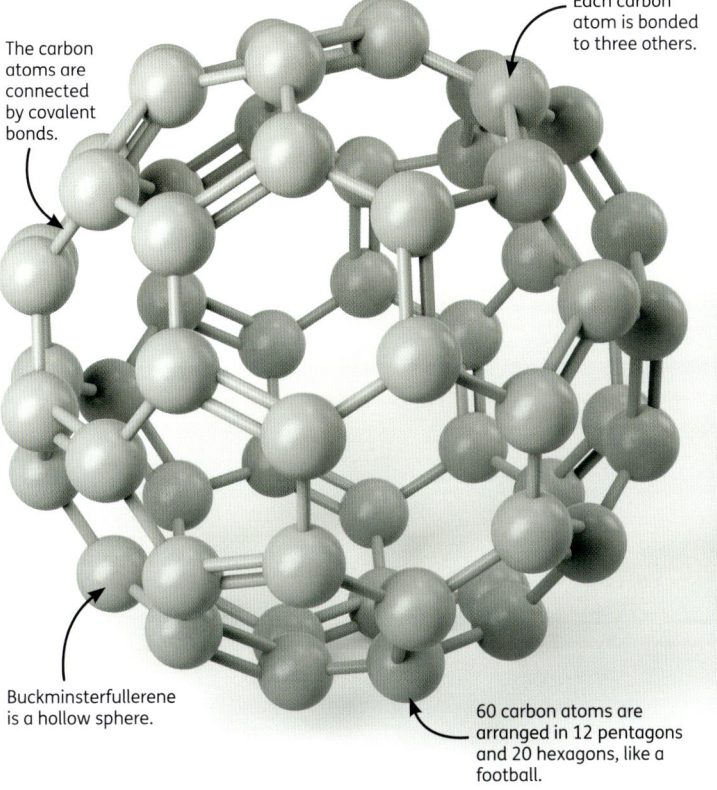

The carbon atoms are connected by covalent bonds.

Each carbon atom is bonded to three others.

Buckminsterfullerene is a hollow sphere.

60 carbon atoms are arranged in 12 pentagons and 20 hexagons, like a football.

RAPPING UP!

Wanna chat about bling? Tell a fella: check **diamond**!
Made out of four carbons all binding, these atoms keep on **combining**, their covalent structures giant.

Here's its chemical structure: no free bonds so it's not a **conductor**.
Bonds so strong, man, it's not gonna rupture.
Thats why it's used in a concrete cutter.

It also has high melting point, high hardness and high density.
Carbon's only diamond when it bonds itself four times not three.

If it bonds itself three times, you have a different **allotrope**.
In this instance it's graphite; don't use the wrong one to propose!

Nanotubes

Nanotube structures, with diameters of mere billionths of a metre, are among the strongest materials known. Their lightness and strength make them ideal for electronics, solar cells and composite materials, like sports equipment.

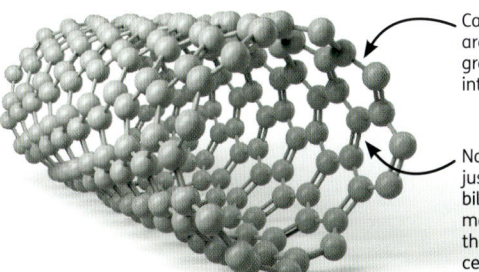

Carbon nanotubes are like a sheet of graphene rolled into a tube.

Nanotubes are just a few billionths of a metre across, but they can be many centimetres long.

Metals

Key facts

- Metals have giant lattice structures (positive metal ions) with delocalised electrons ("a sea" of electrons) that move freely.
- Metals are good conductors of heat and electricity.
- Alloys are a combination of two or more elements; normally metals but can be non-metals like carbon.

Metallic bonding

In metallic substances, electrons in outer shells of metal atoms become delocalised. These electrons can move around positive metal ions. It is these **delocalised electrons** that allow metals to conduct electricity. The electrostatic attraction between the delocalised electrons and metal ions leads to high melting points in most metals.

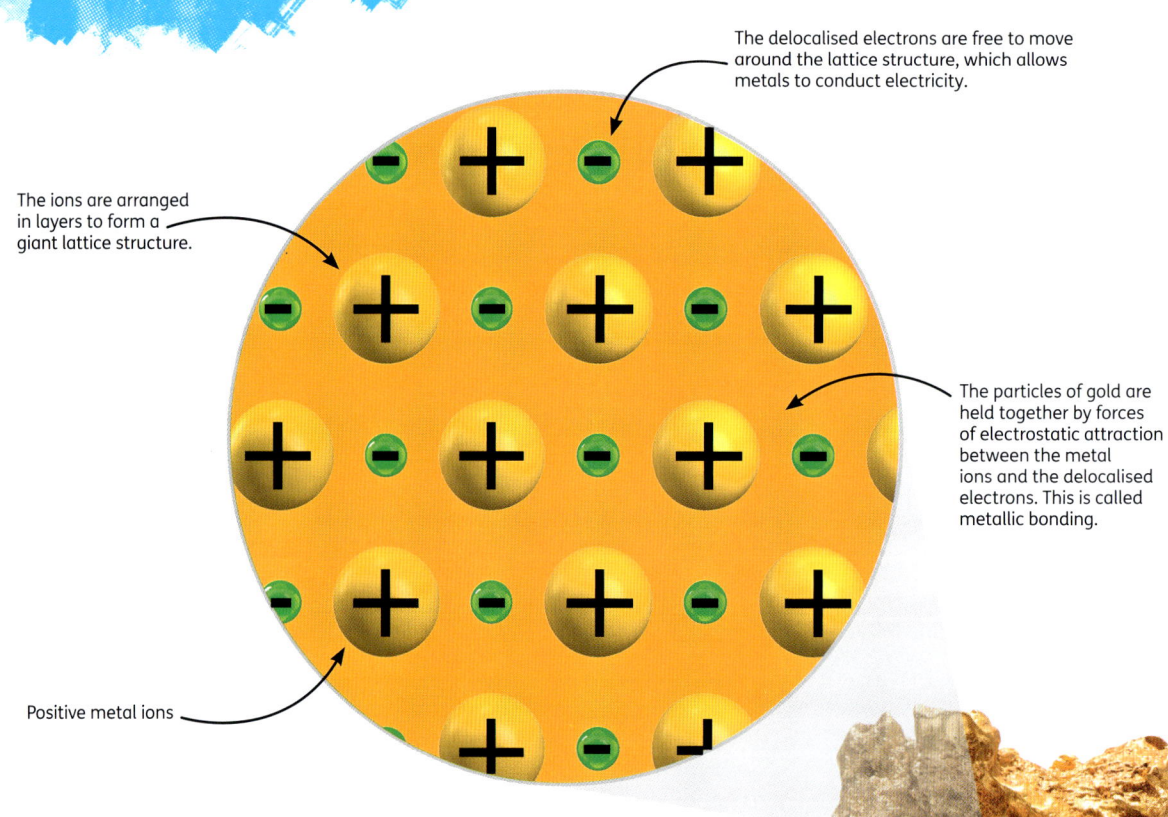

The delocalised electrons are free to move around the lattice structure, which allows metals to conduct electricity.

The ions are arranged in layers to form a giant lattice structure.

The particles of gold are held together by forces of electrostatic attraction between the metal ions and the delocalised electrons. This is called metallic bonding.

Positive metal ions

Conductors of heat and electricity

Metals are excellent conductors of heat and electricity because of the delocalised electrons that are free to move throughout their structure. These delocalised electrons can carry electrical charge or thermal energy quickly through the structure.

Gold is a solid at room temperature – its structure consists of closely packed metal ions.

Bonding, Structure and Properties of Matter

Alloys

An **alloy** combines two or more metals, or sometimes metals with non-metals. Alloys often have different properties from their component elements. Some common examples of alloys include steel, bronze and brass.

Pure metals are often softer than alloys.

Iron

The alloy steel is much harder than pure iron and is often used in construction.

Steel

Alloy hardness

The variation in atomic sizes among different elements increases the difficulty for layers to slide over one another, resulting in **alloys** being harder than pure metals.

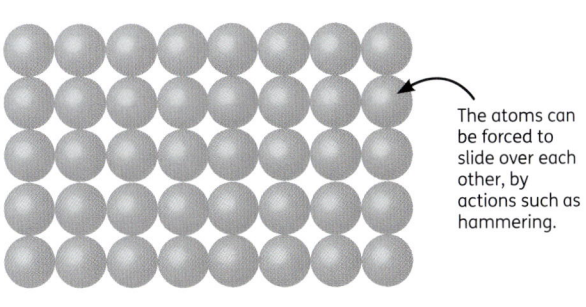

The atoms can be forced to slide over each other, by actions such as hammering.

Pure metal

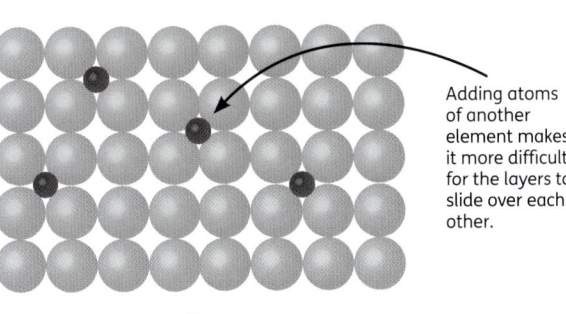

Adding atoms of another element makes it more difficult for the layers to slide over each other.

Alloy

Exam tip

One way to remember the properties of metals is to use the mnemonic **METALS**:

- **M**alleable: metals can be shaped without breaking.
- **E**lectrical conductors: metals are good conductors of electricity because of delocalised electrons.
- **T**hermal conductors: metals are good conductors of heat because of delocalised electrons.
- **A**lloys: alloys can be formed by combining metals with other elements.
- **L**ustrous: metals have a shiny appearance.
- **S**trong: metals are typically strong.

There are always exceptions to this – for example, mercury and the alkali metals are not strong elements with high tensile strength – but most metals adhere to these statements.

Brain Booster

Bonding, Structure and Properties of Matter Recap Quiz

 Find a pen and paper and work through these revision questions.

1. What is an ionic bond?
2. Give an example of a simple molecular substance formed of two different elements.
3. State **two** general properties of ionic compounds.
4. What is the molecular formula of buckminsterfullerene?
5. What is a covalent bond?
6. Explain why graphite can conduct electricity.
7. Why do simple molecular substances generally have low melting and boiling points?
8. Predict the type of bonding in sodium chloride (NaCl).
9. If a substance melts at 1,000°C and conducts electricity in liquid form, what type of bonding do you expect it to have?
10. Explain why ionic compounds conduct electricity when dissolved in water but not in solid form.
11. Compare the electrical conductivity of copper and diamond.
12. Evaluate the possible use of graphene in electronic devices.

Check your answers on page **109**.

Quantitative Chemistry

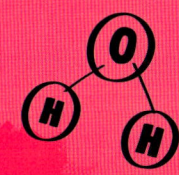

At the end of this chapter, you should be able to:

- ✓ Understand and apply chemical formulae to represent compounds and elements.
- ✓ Balance chemical equations.
- ✓ Calculate the number of moles in a given substance.
- ✓ Calculate the percentage yield of a chemical reaction and evaluate its efficiency.
- ✓ Calculate atom economy of reactions.
- ✓ Identify and correctly use state symbols (s, l, g, aq) in chemical equations.
- ✓ Calculate relative formula mass (M_r) and relative atomic mass (A_r) from given data.
- ✓ Calculate concentrations of solutions.
- ✓ Explain the importance of limiting reactants in chemical reactions.
- ✓ Explain the concept of theoretical yield and how it differs from actual yield in reactions.

Quantitative Chemistry

Formulae

Key facts

- Formulae show the elements found in a compound.
- There are four types of formula: word, chemical, atomic and structural.
- Symbols in equations (s, l, g, aq) indicate the state of matter.

Compounds are created from elements through chemical reactions. These reactions result in the formation of new substances and often involve an observable energy change. Compounds consist of two or more elements chemically combined in fixed proportions and can be represented by formulae using the symbols of the atoms they contain.

Types of formula

Formulae provide an effective and simple means of representing the elements within a compound, utilising words, symbols and occasionally numbers. Various types of **formula** exist. Presented below are four formulae for silicon dioxide:

Word formula
The names of the elements in the compound are listed in full, instead of using their symbols.

Silicon dioxide

Chemical formula
The symbols for each element are used. There is no space between each symbol.

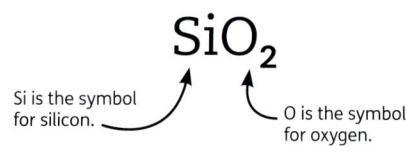
Si is the symbol for silicon. O is the symbol for oxygen.

Atomic formula
The symbols for each element and the outline of each atom show what is in the compound.

O atom

Structural formula
The symbols for each element are connected by a dash that represents a bond between each atom.

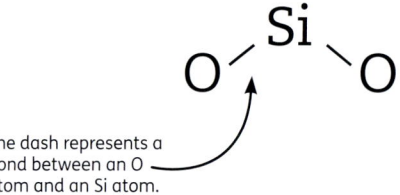
The dash represents a bond between an O atom and an Si atom.

Quantitative Chemistry

Equations

> **Key facts**
> - Equations show reactants changing into products.
> - Equations can use words, symbols or formulae.
> - A balanced equation shows equal atoms on both sides.

Atoms are neither lost nor created during a chemical reaction, so the mass of the products equals the mass of the reactants. Balanced symbol equations show equal numbers of atoms for each element on both sides.

Balancing equations

Equations use symbols to represent chemical reactions. A balanced chemical equation ensures equal numbers of atoms on both sides. Numbers can be added to balance the equation, and charges must also be balanced.

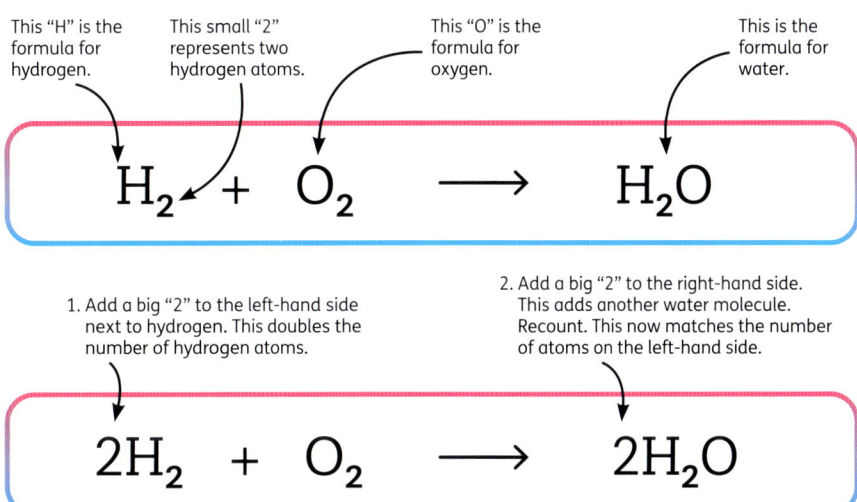

This "H" is the formula for hydrogen.
This small "2" represents two hydrogen atoms.
This "O" is the formula for oxygen.
This is the formula for water.

$$H_2 + O_2 \longrightarrow H_2O$$

1. Add a big "2" to the left-hand side next to hydrogen. This doubles the number of hydrogen atoms.

2. Add a big "2" to the right-hand side. This adds another water molecule. Recount. This now matches the number of atoms on the left-hand side.

$$2H_2 + O_2 \longrightarrow 2H_2O$$

RAPPING UP!

Imma take you through the **formulas** (yeah, that's it) like H_2SO_4 (and $SeCl_6$).
I'll take you through the small number (and prefix).
I'll teach it to you all (here in this remix).

You know, every atom's right here on this table.
Elements – they have a **symbol** on their label.
Starting with the big number (where it's found) it's always on the left (it's for the whole **compound**).

Now where was I before with $SeCl_6$?
You can see there's more than one atom in this.
We need to count the capitals, so please take care to see how many different atoms are in there.

If compounds start to bore you (I'll be quick), H_2O is water (it's no secret).
The H's 2 is smaller (and it means that) there's two Hs in water (and that's a wrap).

Quantitative Chemistry

Relative Masses

Key facts

- The relative atomic mass (A_r) of each element is typically displayed in the periodic table as the larger number next to the chemical symbol.
- Relative formula mass (M_r) of a substance is calculated by finding the sum of the relative atomic mass (A_r) values for all the atoms present in its formula.
- Calculating percentage mass requires using both A_r and M_r values.

Science skills

To calculate the percentage mass of an element in a compound you need to know three values: the element's A_r, the compound's formula and the compound's M_r.

percentage mass of an element =

$$\frac{\text{(atoms of the element)} \times (A_r \text{ of the element})}{M_r \text{ of the compound}}$$

Relative atomic mass (A_r) is a measure of the mass of an atom relative to one-twelfth of the mass of a carbon-12 atom.

Relative formula mass

To calculate the **relative formula mass (M_r)** of a substance, you need to find the sum of the relative atomic mass (A_r) values for all the atoms in its chemical formula. For example, let's calculate the relative formula mass of copper sulfate ($CuSO_4$):

- Find the relative atomic mass of copper (Cu) from the periodic table: $A_r(Cu) = 63.5$
- Find the relative atomic mass of sulfur (S): $A_r(S) = 32$
- Given that there are four oxygen atoms in copper sulfate, multiply the A_r of oxygen by 4:
  $4 \times A_r(O) = 4 \times 16 = 64$
- Add the calculated values together: $M_r(CuSO_4) = 63.5 + 32 + 64 = 159.5$

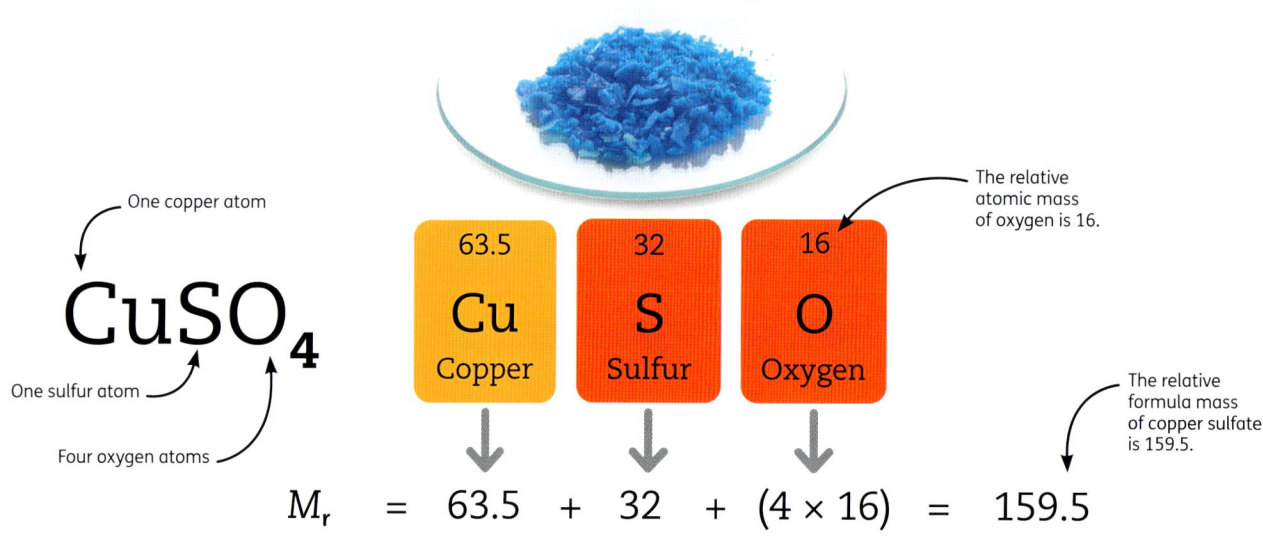

Moles

> **Key facts**
>
> - Quantities of chemicals are measured in moles. The unit is the mole (symbol: "mol").
> - One mole of any substance equals its relative atomic mass (A_r) or relative formula mass (M_r) in grams.
> - The ratio of moles of reactants and products always stays the same.

Moles and the Avogadro constant

Knowing the number of particles (measured in moles) in a substance is crucial. The particles can be atoms, molecules, ions or electrons.

Question
How many moles in 36 g of carbon?

Answer
There is 1 mole in 12 g so there are 3 moles in 36 g.

Moles and equations

By knowing the number of moles, we can predict how much of each substance is needed or produced in a reaction using the balanced equation. We can calculate the relative masses of substances involved and ensure the reaction is carried out with the correct proportions.

RAPPING UP!

First things first, I'm explaining the term,
I'm breaking it down now just wait, and you'll learn.
The **mole's** an amount like a paycheck you earn,
but you ain't working yet so that ain't ya concern.

Working with atoms the term's a breakthrough;
it simplifies things so you won't be confused.
If a dozen means 12 and a pair means 2,
how much is a mole? Now the number is huge.

I'll tell you right now what it's meant to be:
it's six times ten to the twenty-three.
That's the number of atoms that one mole amounts;
using this term makes it easier to count.

I'm telling you now it's essential you know,
the mole's inventor was called **Avogadro**.
This number right here? It's time that I show
this number in grams means that you then
have one mole.

Just look at carbon; it's 12 on this spot.
Have 12 grams of carbon it's one mole you've got.
Have 24 grams? I'll leave that to you.
You getting the maths? Coz the answer is two.

Two moles of **carbon** is how many **atoms**?
Times 2 by this number and tell me what happens.
I'm glad that you got this; I'm not teaching Latin.
I'm good in the class but on beat an assassin!

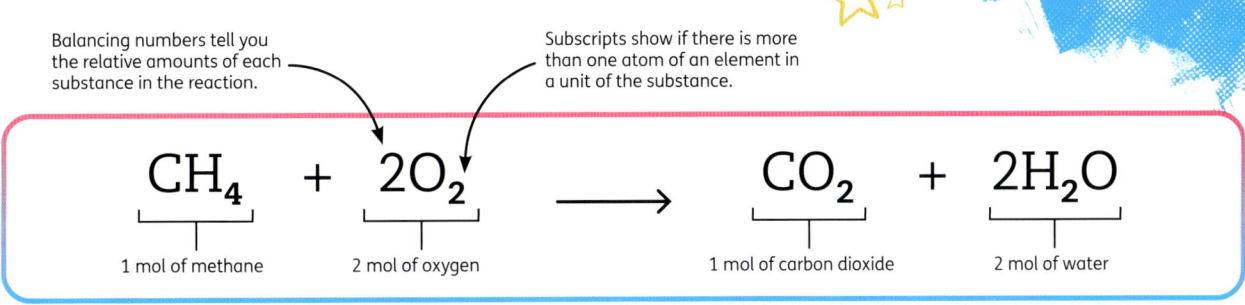

Balancing numbers tell you the relative amounts of each substance in the reaction.

Subscripts show if there is more than one atom of an element in a unit of the substance.

$$CH_4 + 2O_2 \longrightarrow CO_2 + 2H_2O$$

1 mol of methane • 2 mol of oxygen • 1 mol of carbon dioxide • 2 mol of water

$$C + O_2 \longrightarrow CO_2$$

Chemical Calculations

Key facts

- Reactions often yield multiple products, including useful ones and waste ones.
- Atom economy measures how efficiently reactants form a product; higher atom economy means less waste.
- Enhancing the atom economy of a reaction can be achieved by identifying applications for waste products.
- Actual yield is the mass produced in a reaction.
- Theoretical yield is the maximum possible mass that can be produced.
- Percentage yield ranges from 0 per cent (no product) to 100 per cent (maximum product).
- In chemical reactions, mass is conserved.

Science skills

The atom economy of a reaction represents the proportion of atoms from the reactants that are incorporated into the desired product. It is calculated using the following equation:

percentage atom economy =

$$\frac{\text{total } M_r \text{ of the desired product}}{\text{total } M_r \text{ of all reactants}} \times 100$$

Percentage yield

Percentage yield is the ratio of the actual yield of a product to the theoretical yield, expressed as a percentage. It helps to evaluate the efficiency of a chemical reaction by comparing the amount of product actually obtained to the maximum possible amount predicted by stoichiometric calculations. Factors such as incomplete reactions, side reactions and losses during purification can affect the percentage yield. Actual yields are always less than 100 per cent.

Atom economy

Evaluating a chemical process can be done by calculating its **atom economy**. This efficiency measure assesses the conversion of reactants into a desired product. Often, chemical processes result in not only the intended product but also additional by-products.

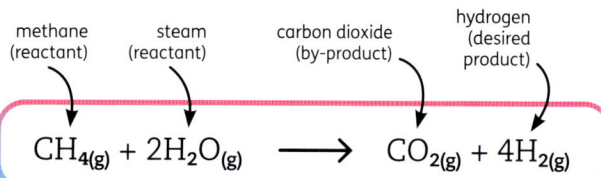

$$CH_{4(g)} + 2H_2O_{(g)} \longrightarrow CO_{2(g)} + 4H_{2(g)}$$

methane (reactant), steam (reactant), carbon dioxide (by-product), hydrogen (desired product)

In this reaction, the hydrogen gas is the desired product. To determine the atom economy of the reaction, determine the M_r of the reactants and hydrogen. Carbon dioxide can be omitted as it is not wanted. This gives a total M_r for the reactants of 52 and for hydrogen of 8. Putting the values obtained into the equation:

$$\frac{8}{52} \times 100 = 15.4\%$$

Conservation of mass

The **law of conservation of mass** states that the total mass remains constant during a reaction, as no atoms are created or destroyed. Therefore, a balanced chemical equation has equal numbers of each type of atom on each side.

Colourless silver nitrate solution.

Orange potassium dichromate solution.

Cloudy orange–brown precipitate in the reaction mixture.

The total mass of the flask, measuring cylinder, and reaction mixture stays the same.

The equation shown illustrates the reaction between magnesium and chlorine when heated, resulting in the formation of magnesium chloride. The reaction involves the separation and recombination of atoms without creating or destroying any atoms.

magnesium
Mg

There is one magnesium atom at the start of the reaction.

chlorine
Cl_2

There are two chlorine atoms at the start of the reaction.

magnesium chloride
$MgCl_2$

The number of atoms is the same at the start and end of the reaction.

Some reactions in a science laboratory may appear to conflict with the law of conservation as they get lighter or heavier. This is because during the chemical reactions gases either escape or enter open containers. The law of conservation of mass is still in effect; you just have to think more carefully about what is happening.

Exam tip

The total mass of reactants equals the total mass of products. In a sealed reaction vessel, the mass remains unchanged. If the vessel is open, the mass can vary.

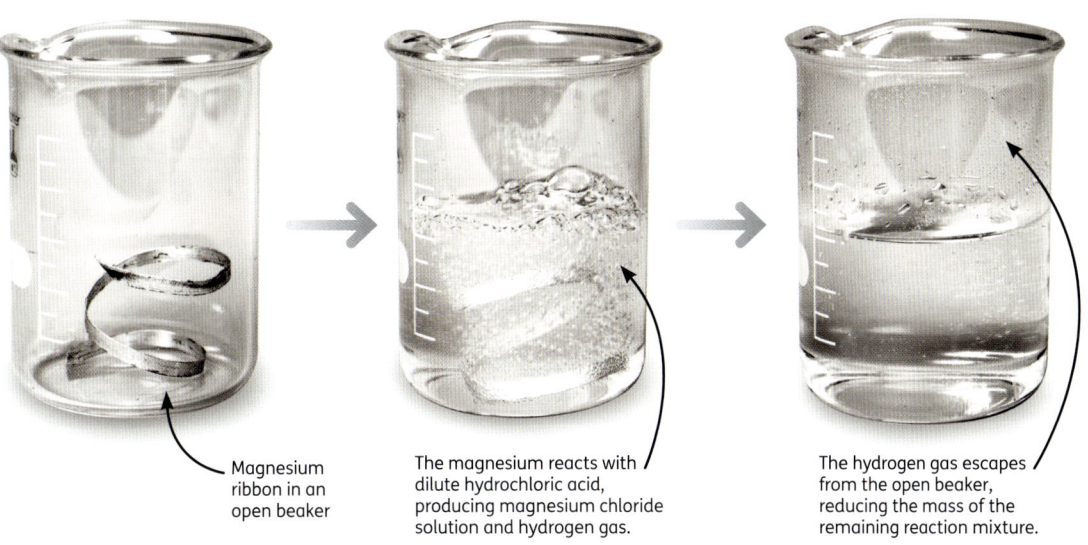

Magnesium ribbon in an open beaker

The magnesium reacts with dilute hydrochloric acid, producing magnesium chloride solution and hydrogen gas.

The hydrogen gas escapes from the open beaker, reducing the mass of the remaining reaction mixture.

32 Brain Booster

Quantitative Chemistry Recap Quiz

 Find a pen and paper and work through these revision questions. You will need access to a periodic table for some of the questions.

1. Calculate the relative formula mass of H_2O.
2. Calculate the number of moles in 88 g of CO_2.
3. What is the mass of 2 moles of NaCl?
4. Explain the law of conservation of mass.
5. If 10 g of reactant A reacts with 15 g of reactant B to form product C, what is the mass of product C?
6. Calculate the percentage yield if 20 g of product are produced from a theoretical yield of 25 g.
7. If the theoretical yield was 50 g and the percentage yield of the reaction was 90 per cent, what was the actual yield obtained?
8. Define atom economy and explain its importance in green chemistry.
9. Calculate the atom economy for the formation of water (H_2O) from hydrogen (H_2) and oxygen (O_2).
10. How is the relative formula mass of a molecule determined using the periodic table?
11. What is the mass of 0.5 moles of $CaCO_3$?
12. Calculate the number of moles in 144 g of carbon.
13. If you have 3 moles of H_2SO_4, what is the mass?

Check your answers on page **109**.

Chemical Changes

At the end of this chapter, you should be able to:

- ✓ State the position of key metals in the reactivity series.
- ✓ Describe the general properties and characteristics of metals in various positions of the reactivity series.
- ✓ Explain the relationship between metal reactivity and the formation of positive ions.
- ✓ Evaluate the environmental impact of metal extraction techniques.
- ✓ State the main steps involved in extracting metals from their ores.
- ✓ Describe the process of electrolysis and its applications in metal extraction.
- ✓ State the definition of acids, bases and neutralisation.
- ✓ Describe how acids and bases react to form salts and water.
- ✓ Explain how to perform a titration experiment to determine the concentration of an acid or a base.
- ✓ Describe neutralisation reactions.

Chemical Changes

The Reactivity Series

Key facts

- Some elements are more chemically reactive than others.
- A reactivity series ranks elements by their tendency to lose electrons during reactions.
- Elements that easily lose electrons are at the top; those that don't are at the bottom.
- The list is mainly made up of metals but can also include some non-metals like hydrogen and carbon.

List of elements

A metal's reactivity depends on its tendency to form **positive ions**. Use the words to the left of the elements to help you remember them.

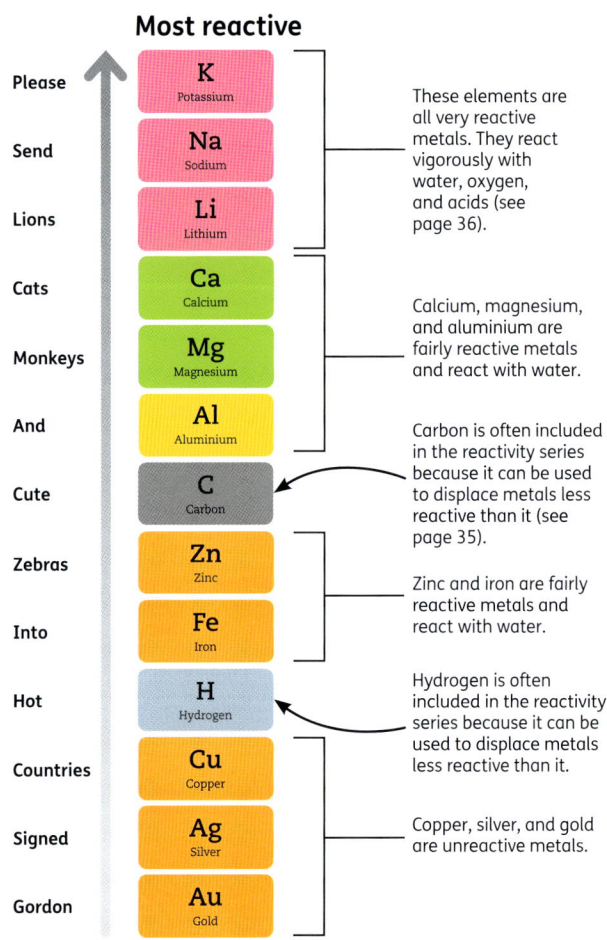

The **reactivity series** is an ordered list of elements. The most reactive elements are at the top and the least reactive at the bottom.

RAPPING UP!

What's featured here in these theories?
The **reactivity** series.
Learn what's next and don't feel too weary;
memorise this – it goes like...

Please send lions, cats, monkeys
and cute zebras into hot countries,
signed Gordon – yeah, that sounds funky,
but now its stored in ya head real comfy.

How do **metals** react with water?
Potassium, well it just slaughters,
and sodium, yeah, it still falters.
Lithium less and calcium poorer.

And how do they react with acid?
Well, calcium's actually quite quick,
and **magnesium** after is still slick;
iron reacts more slowly than zinc.

As for copper, silver and gold,
well, they're all reactively cold.
A fact right there it really makes sense:
one is bling and the other one's pence.

You wouldn't want your jewellery corroding
or the water pipes in ya house exploding.
There's more to this that needs knowing;
give me one sec cos I need reloading.

Metal plus **water** – it goes to them:
metal hydroxide and hydrogen.
Metal plus **acid** – don't be at fault:
makes H_2, but also makes **salt**.

And finally, we're on to displacement;
that's a fancy word for replacement.
This couple breaks their engagement;
this one's dropped right down to the pavement.

Extraction of Metals

Key facts

- Metal oxides are produced when metals react with oxygen.
- Metals that are less reactive than carbon (such as iron and copper) can be extracted from their ores using carbon, though the results are not very pure.
- Reduction means the removal of oxygen. Oxidation means the addition of oxygen.

Unreactive metals are found in their natural (**native**) state. However, most metals exist as compounds which are less useful than the pure metal.
To extract the pure metal, oxygen is removed from the compound in a process called **reduction**. Metals less reactive than carbon can be extracted from their oxides by reducing them with carbon. The opposite process to reduction is adding oxygen. This is called **oxidation**.

Blast furnace

Iron extraction involves a high-temperature reaction, where heated iron ore and carbon compounds are placed in large containers.

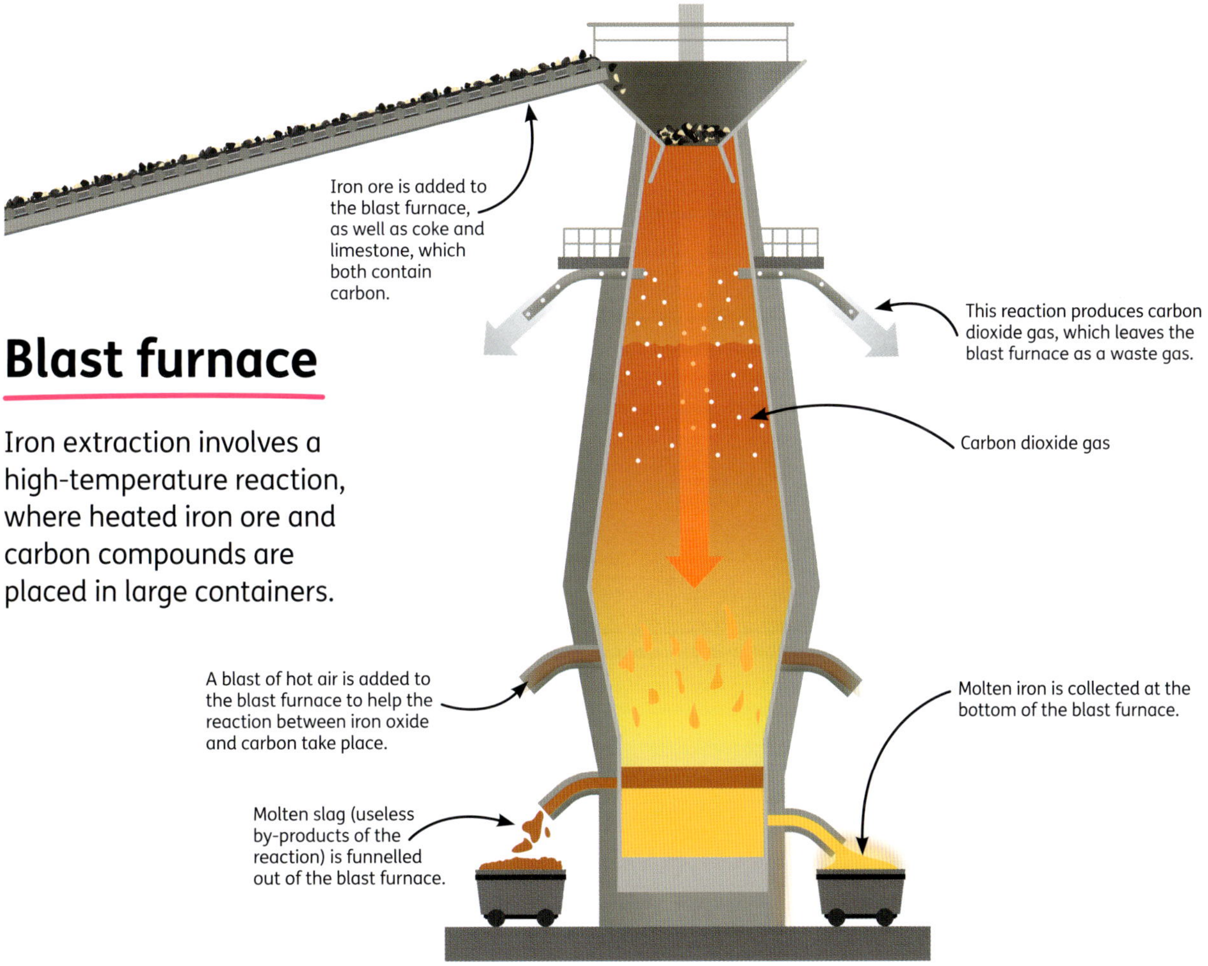

- Iron ore is added to the blast furnace, as well as coke and limestone, which both contain carbon.
- This reaction produces carbon dioxide gas, which leaves the blast furnace as a waste gas.
- Carbon dioxide gas
- A blast of hot air is added to the blast furnace to help the reaction between iron oxide and carbon take place.
- Molten iron is collected at the bottom of the blast furnace.
- Molten slag (useless by-products of the reaction) is funnelled out of the blast furnace.

iron oxide	+	carbon	→	iron	+	carbon dioxide
$2Fe_2O_3$	+	$3C$	→	$4Fe$	+	$3CO_2$

Chemical Changes

Metals and Acids

Key facts

- Certain metals react more strongly with acids compared to other metals.
- A salt is produced when a metal reacts with an acid.
- A salt is a chemical compound resulting from the complete or partial substitution of hydrogen ions in an acid with metal ions (or ammonium ions).

Exam tip

To remember the general reaction for metals with acid, use the acronym **MASH**:

metal + **a**cid → **s**alt + **h**ydrogen

Metals at the top of the reactivity series react vigorously with acids at room temperature. In these reactions, metals lose electrons and produce a **metal salt solution** and **hydrogen gas**.

Metals reacting with acids

The most common products of a metal reacting with an acid are a salt and hydrogen. The hydrogen gas produced can be seen as fizzing, and this shows how reactive a metal is. Magnesium vigorously reacts with acid, producing many bubbles of hydrogen, unlike lead, which does not seem to react at all.

If the acid used is **hydrochloric acid** (HCl), a **chloride** salt is produced. **Sulfuric acid** (H_2SO_4) makes **sulfate** salts, and **nitrate** salts are the products when **nitric acid** (HNO_3) is used.

Lots of hydrogen gas bubbles are produced when magnesium reacts with hydrochloric acid.

Only a few hydrogen gas bubbles are produced when an iron screw is placed in hydrochloric acid.

Magnesium   **Zinc**   **Iron**   **Lead**

Chemical Changes

Neutralisation Reactions

The pH scale

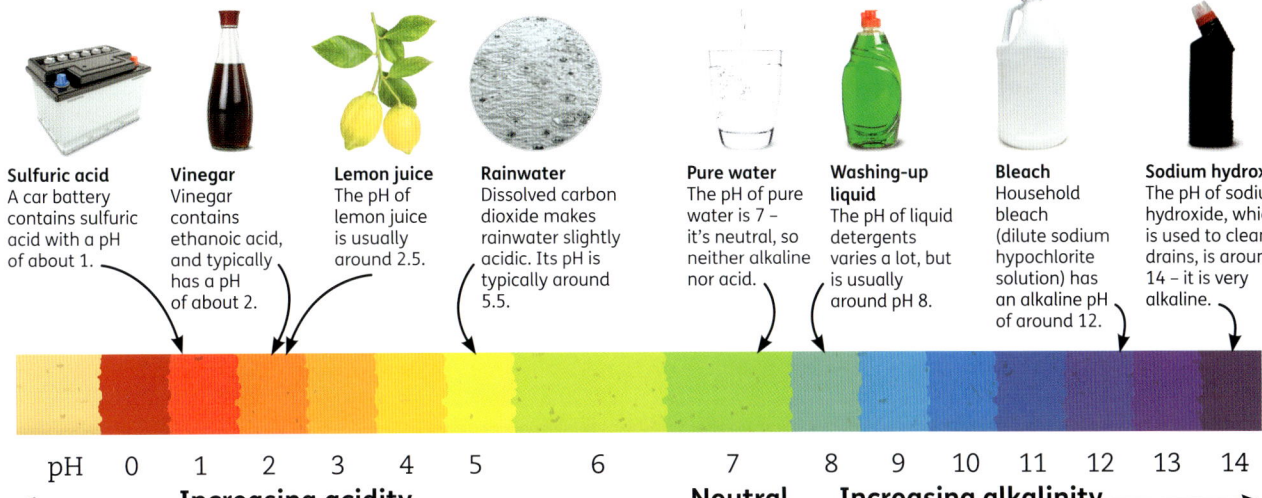

Sulfuric acid
A car battery contains sulfuric acid with a pH of about 1.

Vinegar
Vinegar contains ethanoic acid, and typically has a pH of about 2.

Lemon juice
The pH of lemon juice is usually around 2.5.

Rainwater
Dissolved carbon dioxide makes rainwater slightly acidic. Its pH is typically around 5.5.

Pure water
The pH of pure water is 7 – it's neutral, so neither alkaline nor acid.

Washing-up liquid
The pH of liquid detergents varies a lot, but is usually around pH 8.

Bleach
Household bleach (dilute sodium hypochlorite solution) has an alkaline pH of around 12.

Sodium hydroxide
The pH of sodium hydroxide, which is used to clean drains, is around 14 – it is very alkaline.

pH 0 1 2 3 4 5 6 7 8 9 10 11 12 13 14
← Increasing acidity   Neutral   Increasing alkalinity →

Key facts

- A base is a substance that can neutralise an acid. Bases have a pH greater than 7. Alkalis are soluble bases.
- In aqueous solutions, acids produce hydrogen ions (H^+) and alkalis produce hydroxide ions (OH^-).
- Neutralisation is a reaction between an acid and a base.

Neutralisation

When equal quantities of acid and base react in a **neutralisation** reaction, the resulting **neutral** solution has a pH of 7. The products of this reaction are a salt and water. The type of salt formed depends on the acid and base.

Making soluble salts

To obtain a pure sample of a **soluble salt**, you add excess base to a specific volume of acid. Using an excess of base ensures all the acid has reacted. You filter the resulting solution to remove the insoluble base; the soluble salt will pass through. You heat the resulting filtrate to evaporate the water.

RAPPING UP!

You wanna know what **pH** is?
It's a scale, no need to wonder.
Shows if **acidic** or basic.
Look right here and check out this number.

First let's start with acids.
1 is strong and 6 is weak.
If below 3 then it's a hazard,
pH meter here's the technique.

Now for 8 to 14
that means it's an **alkali**.
14s strong and 8 is weak.
Neutral's central not low, not high.

For colour change we use a dye –
that Universal **indicator**.
All the colors? We got some time
gonna list them right now and not later.

Red and purple – they're the extremes.
If they gets on your skin then
you'll let out scream.
In the middle, neutral is green.
Orange and yellow and blue in between.

A base that dissolves is an alkali.
Just in case you did not yet realise.
Mix acid with base you get a surprise.
H plus and OH minus – **neutralise**.

Acids and Titrations

In chemistry, "strong" and "weak" have specific definitions. Acids ionise in water into hydrogen ions (H^+) and anions (negative ions). Strong acids fully ionise in water, whereas weak acids only **partially ionise**. Remember the strength of the acid is not the same as the concentration.

Key facts

- Acids ionise (dissociate) in water to produce positive hydrogen ions (H^+).
- Strong and weak refer to how ionised an acid is in water.
- Dilute and concentrated refer to the amount of acid dissolved in the solution.
- Titration is a technique that can be used to determine the concentration of an unknown solution.

Strong and weak acids

Strong acids ionise fully into H^+ ions and anions. Weak acids only partially ionise, releasing fewer H^+ ions.

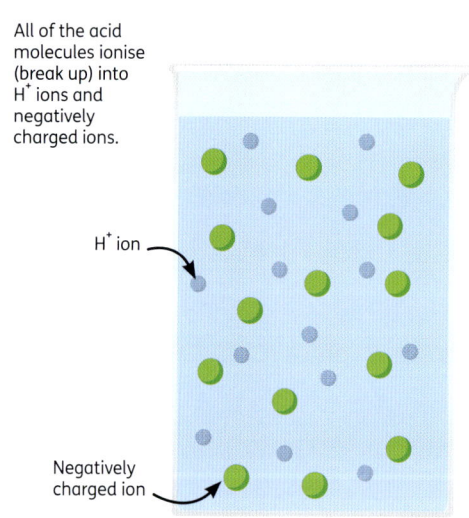

All of the acid molecules ionise (break up) into H^+ ions and negatively charged ions.

H^+ ion

Negatively charged ion

Strong acid

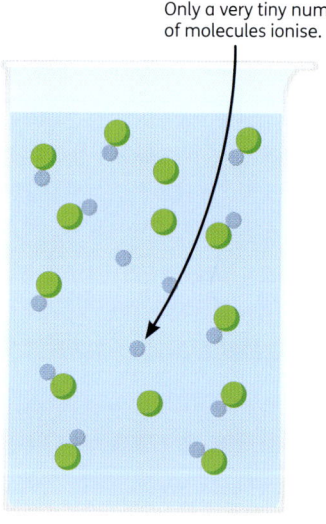

Only a very tiny number of molecules ionise.

Weak acid

Dilute and concentrated acids

A **dilute acid solution** has fewer acid molecules compared to water, while a **concentrated acid solution** has more. "Strong" and "weak" refer to the ionisation level of acids in water, whereas "dilute" and "concentrated" refer to the amount of acid dissolved. A weak acid can be either concentrated or dilute, and the same applies to strong acids. The danger of an acid depends on its concentration and its strength.

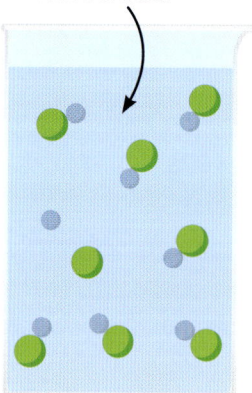

There is a low ratio of acid molecules to volume of water.

Dilute solution of a weak acid

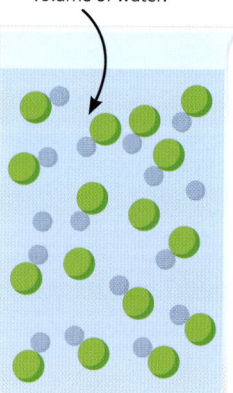

There is a higher ratio of acid molecules to volume of water.

Concentrated solution of a weak acid

Chemical Changes

Titrations

Titration is a method used to determine the concentration of an unknown solution (acid or alkali) by reacting it with a solution of known concentration. An **indicator** is added to observe the colour change, and the amount of solution required to cause this change is recorded. This is called the **end-point**.

The long piece of glassware in the picture is called a burette. It is used to measure very small volumes. Burettes are normally marked with 0 cm³ at the top and 50 cm³ at the bottom to make calculations easier.

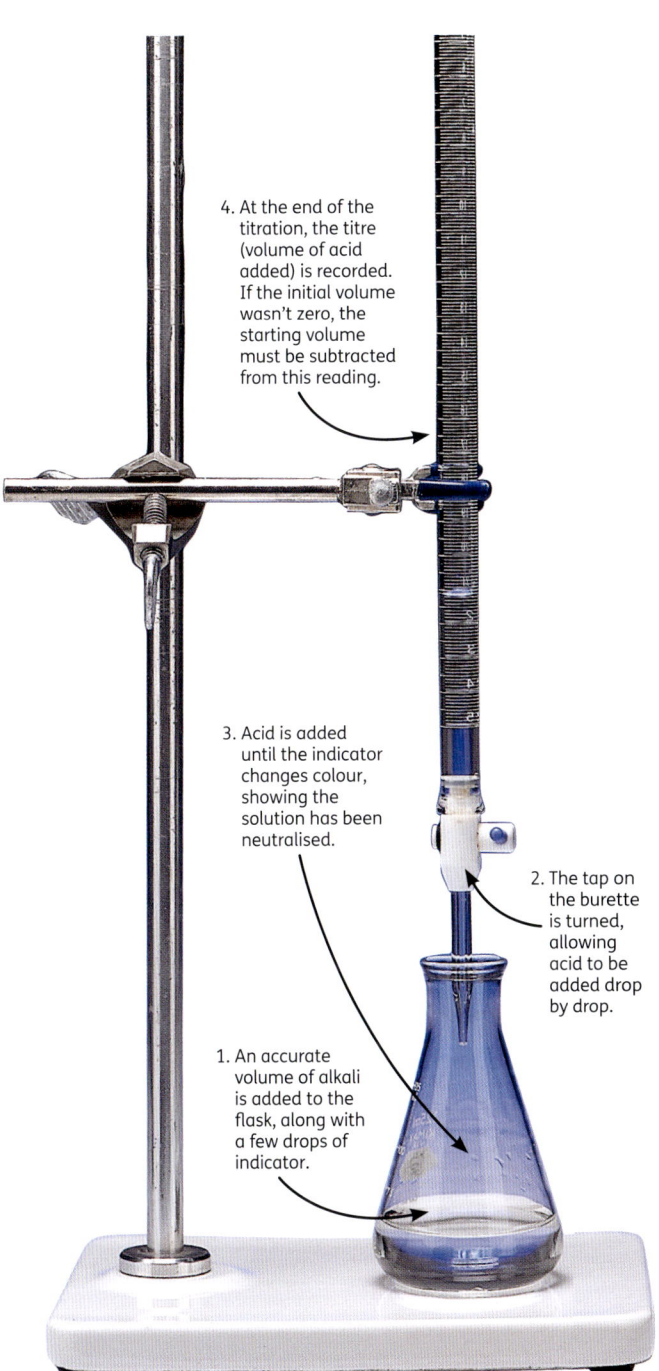

4. At the end of the titration, the titre (volume of acid added) is recorded. If the initial volume wasn't zero, the starting volume must be subtracted from this reading.

3. Acid is added until the indicator changes colour, showing the solution has been neutralised.

2. The tap on the burette is turned, allowing acid to be added drop by drop.

1. An accurate volume of alkali is added to the flask, along with a few drops of indicator.

Science skills

In titration, the concentration of one solution is known while the other's is unknown. By knowing the reacting volumes, you can calculate the unknown concentration. Use the following equation:

concentration (mol/dm^3) =

$$\frac{\text{amount of solute (mol)}}{\text{volume of solution (dm}^3\text{)}}$$

For example, in the reaction
$HCl + NaOH \rightarrow NaCl + H_2O$
25 cm³ of 0.1 mol/dm³ hydrochloric acid neutralises 30 cm³ of a sodium hydroxide solution. To calculate the concentration of the sodium hydroxide solution:

1. Convert the volumes to dm³ by dividing each value by 1,000.

   25 cm³ = 0.025 dm³
   30 cm³ = 0.030 dm³

2. Calculate the mol of hydrochloric acid (HCl) present.

   Amount of HCl = 0.025 dm³ × 0.1 ml/dm³

   = 0.0025 mol

3. From the equation, 1mol of HCl reacts with 1mol of NaOH. So, this means 0.0025mol of HCl reacts with 0.0025mol of NaOH.

   conc. of NaOH = $\frac{0.0025}{0.030}$

   concentration of NaOH = 0.083 mol/dm³

Chemical Changes

Electrolysis

Electrolysis involves using an electric current to separate compounds into their constituent elements. This process is applied in industry to obtain **pure metals**. For electrolysis to function, ions need to be able to move freely, which means a substance needs to be dissolved in a solution (for example, water) or in its molten (liquid) state. The substance in its molten state or dissolved form is referred to as the **electrolyte**.

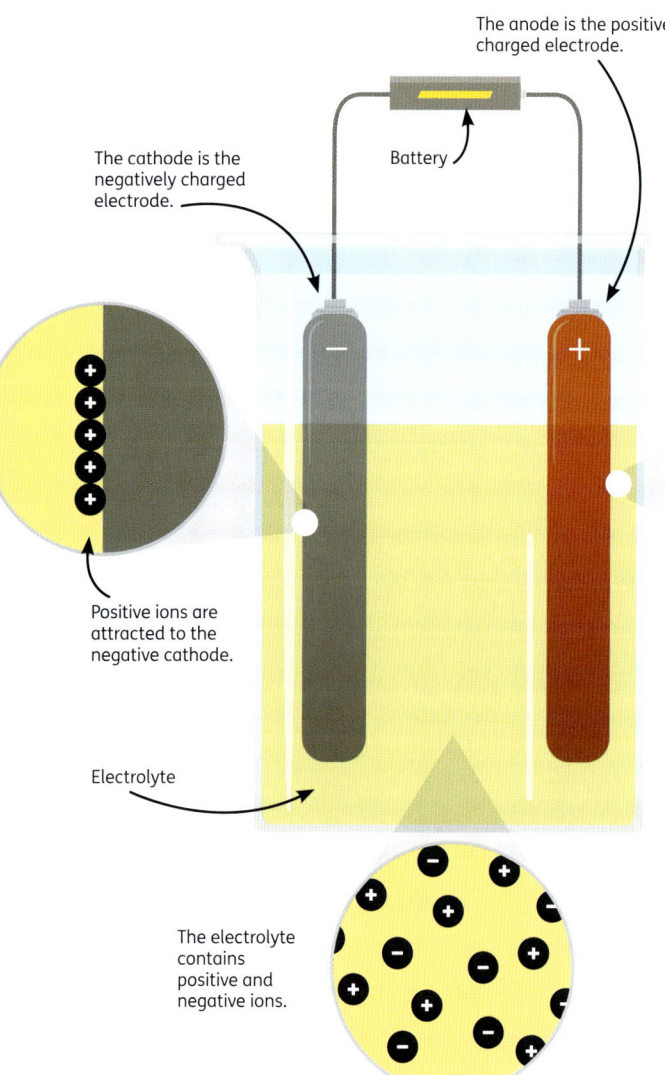

The anode is the positively charged electrode.

Battery

The cathode is the negatively charged electrode.

Positive ions are attracted to the negative cathode.

Electrolyte

The electrolyte contains positive and negative ions.

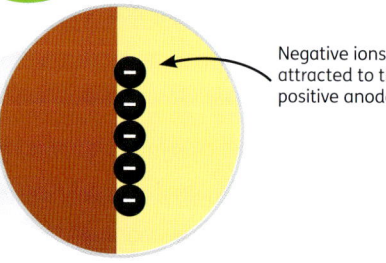

Negative ions are attracted to the positive anode.

RAPPING UP!

Some call this topic the worst, but I'll sum it all up in one verse. Let's go, so first things first, I'll start by describing the word.

Electro comes from electron; and lysis means to split. A great teacher – it's time you met one, I'll break this down bit by bit.

You're thinking, "Why should I know this?" Your phone and your PlayStation? You can't have them without this **process**, and notice they made from metals.

And those **metals** have to be found; you find them as ores in the ground. And we've got to make them pure – almost as pure as this sound.

Not there yet? You'll come round. Take a well-known metal **compound** – copper chloride is renowned – to make pure, I'll tell you how.

Anions negative like onions, cations positive like cats, anodes take away electrons, and cathodes give them back.

Exam tip

In electrolysis, half equations represent the processes occurring at the cathode and anode. For example, in electrolysis of molten sodium chloride, the half equation at the cathode is $Na^+ + e^- \rightarrow Na$, showing the reduction of sodium ions. Conversely, the half equation at the anode is $2Cl^- \rightarrow Cl_2 + 2e^-$, which represents the oxidation of chloride ions.

Chemical Changes

Key facts

- Electrolysis involves using electricity to decompose compounds.
- Electrolysis is used in industry to obtain pure metals.
- The substance being electrolysed must be either molten or dissolved in a solution.
- Half equations describe the reactions at each electrode during electrolysis.
- Electrolysis splits water into H^+ and OH^- ions, producing hydrogen gas (H_2) and oxygen gas (O_2).

Electrolysis of aqueous solutions

Electrolysis is capable of separating a substance when it is dissolved in water, forming an **aqueous solution**. During this process, hydrogen ions (H^+) and hydroxide ions (OH^-), along with other elements, are drawn to the respective **electrodes**.

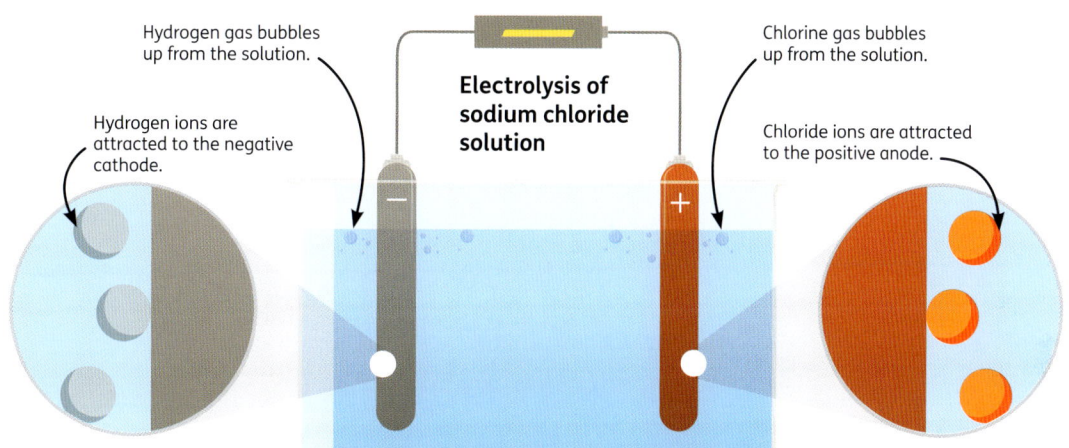

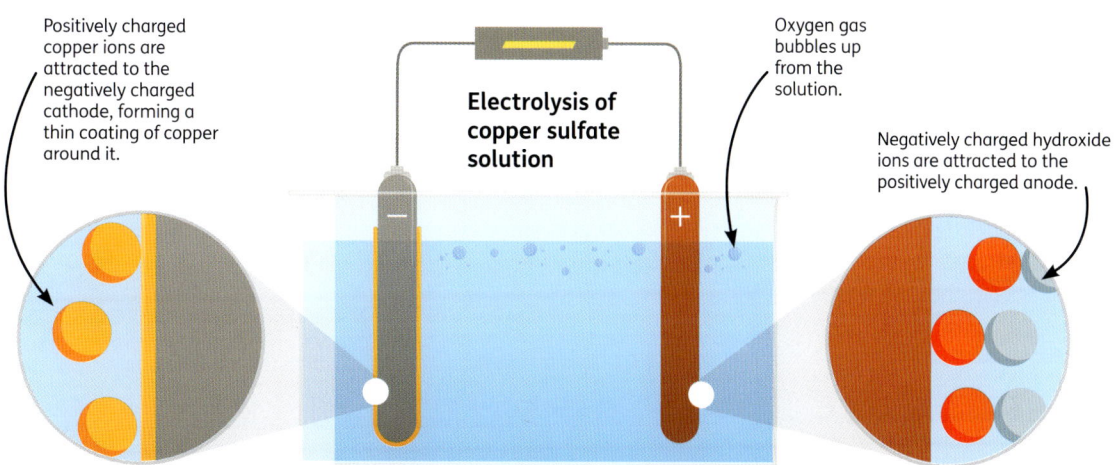

At the **cathode**, hydrogen is produced if the metal is more reactive than hydrogen. At the anode, oxygen is produced unless halide ions are present, in which case the halogen is produced. This competition for the electrodes occurs because the water molecules also break down into hydrogen ions and hydroxide ions in an aqueous solution.

42 Brain Booster

Chemical Changes Recap Quiz

 Find a pen and paper and work through these revision questions. You will need access to a periodic table for some of the questions.

1. State the general reaction formula for the reaction between a metal and an acid.
2. Describe the reactivity series of metals.
3. Explain the process of electrolysis in molten sodium chloride.
4. Identify the products formed at the cathode and anode during electrolysis of aqueous sodium chloride solution.
5. Compare strong acids and weak acids in terms of ionisation in water.
6. State the pH range for acidic solutions.
7. Describe the process of titration used to determine the concentration of an acid or a base.
8. Explain how soluble salts are produced from acids and insoluble bases.
9. Identify the ions present in an aqueous solution of sodium chloride.
10. List **three** strong acids and their chemical formulae.
11. Describe what happens when a metal reacts with oxygen.
12. Explain the term "oxidation" in a chemical reaction.

Check your answers on page **109**.

Energy Changes

At the end of this chapter, you should be able to:

- ✓ State the definition of exothermic and endothermic reactions.
- ✓ List examples of exothermic and endothermic reactions in everyday life.
- ✓ Describe the energy changes that occur during exothermic reactions.
- ✓ Describe the energy changes that occur during endothermic reactions.
- ✓ Calculate the energy change in a reaction using bond energy values.
- ✓ State the function of chemical cells and fuel cells.
- ✓ List the advantages and disadvantages of different types of fuel cell.
- ✓ Explain how chemical cells generate electricity.
- ✓ Calculate the voltage produced by a chemical cell.
- ✓ State the applications of chemical cells and fuel cells in real-world scenarios.
- ✓ Describe the chemical reactions that occur in a hydrogen fuel cell.

Energy Changes

Exothermic and Endothermic Reactions

Key facts

- Exothermic reactions transfer energy – mainly heat – to the surroundings, raising the temperature.
- Common exothermic reactions include combustion, neutralisation and displacement.
- Endothermic reactions absorb energy from the surroundings, requiring continuous energy supply.
- Endothermic reactions lower the temperature of the reaction mixtures.
- Examples of endothermic reactions are thermal decomposition, photosynthesis and electrolysis.

Exothermic reactions

Reactions can be **exothermic** or **endothermic**. Exothermic reactions **transfer energy to the surroundings**, raising the temperature. An example is fuel combustion.

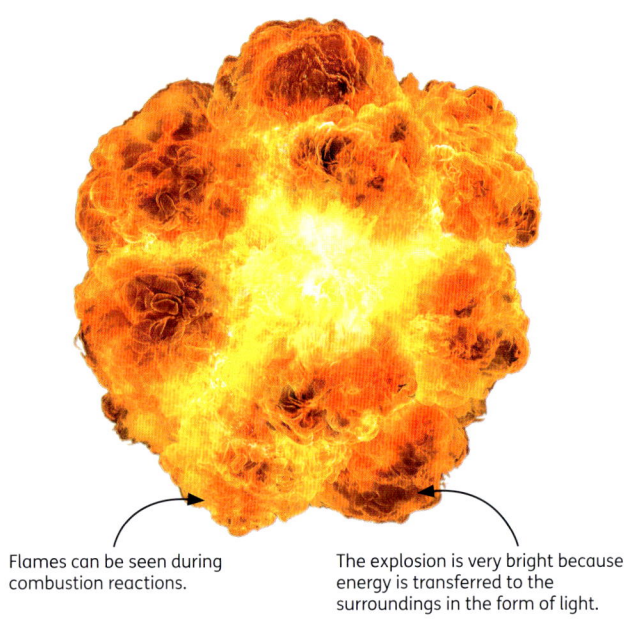

Flames can be seen during combustion reactions.

The explosion is very bright because energy is transferred to the surroundings in the form of light.

How exothermic reactions work

1. Potassium is added to water and produces potassium hydroxide and hydrogen gas.

2. Increased heating occurs, causing the hydrogen to ignite with a lilac flame.

3. The hot metal gives off sparks and disappears with a small explosion at the end of the reaction.

Energy Changes

Endothermic reactions

An endothermic reaction involves the transfer of energy from the surroundings to the reacting substances, resulting in a decrease in the temperature of the solution when the reactions occur in solutions. While chemical reactions can be either exothermic or endothermic, endothermic reactions are less common. Examples of endothermic reactions include photosynthesis, thermal decomposition reactions and electrolysis.

How endothermic reactions work

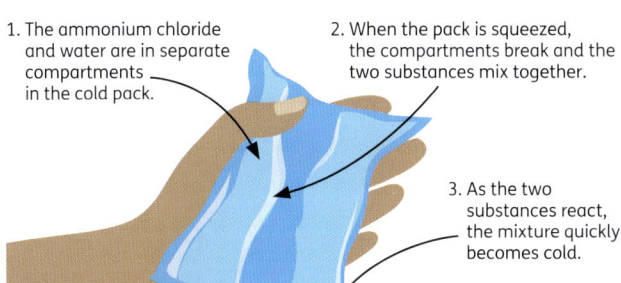

1. The ammonium chloride and water are in separate compartments in the cold pack.
2. When the pack is squeezed, the compartments break and the two substances mix together.
3. As the two substances react, the mixture quickly becomes cold.

Sodium hydrogen carbonate powder is added to the solution.

Bubbles of carbon dioxide are given off during the reaction.

A dilute acid, such as citric acid, is added to the sodium hydrogen carbonate.

The temperature of the reaction mixture goes down.

RAPPING UP!

Exothermic and endothermic reactions are different chemical reactions that can happen. If the temperature increases, then its **exothermic**. Think of when you light a match, you strike it and burn it.

Exothermic reactions release heat so the chemical energy **depletes**. Into the surroundings it is released so the temperature goes up when it is complete.

Endothermic is the opposite – it gets cool. Energy is taken in by all the chemicals. Temperature **lowers** I can confirm it. It's like me – the reaction here is **endothermic**.

Energy Changes

Reaction Profiles

Key facts

- In exothermic reactions, the energy level of the reactants is higher than that of the products. The activation energy is indicated by an upward arrow that exceeds the energy level of the reactants. The overall energy change is represented by a downward arrow.
- In endothermic reactions, the energy level of the products is higher than that of the reactants. The activation energy is indicated by an upward arrow that exceeds the energy level of the products. The overall energy change is represented by an upward arrow.

Bond-breaking and bond-making

Bond-forming is an exothermic process as it releases energy, while **bond-breaking** is an endothermic process as it requires energy. During exothermic reactions, more energy is released when bonds form in the products than is needed to break bonds in the reactants. Conversely, in endothermic reactions, more energy is required to break bonds in the reactants than is released when bonds form in the products.

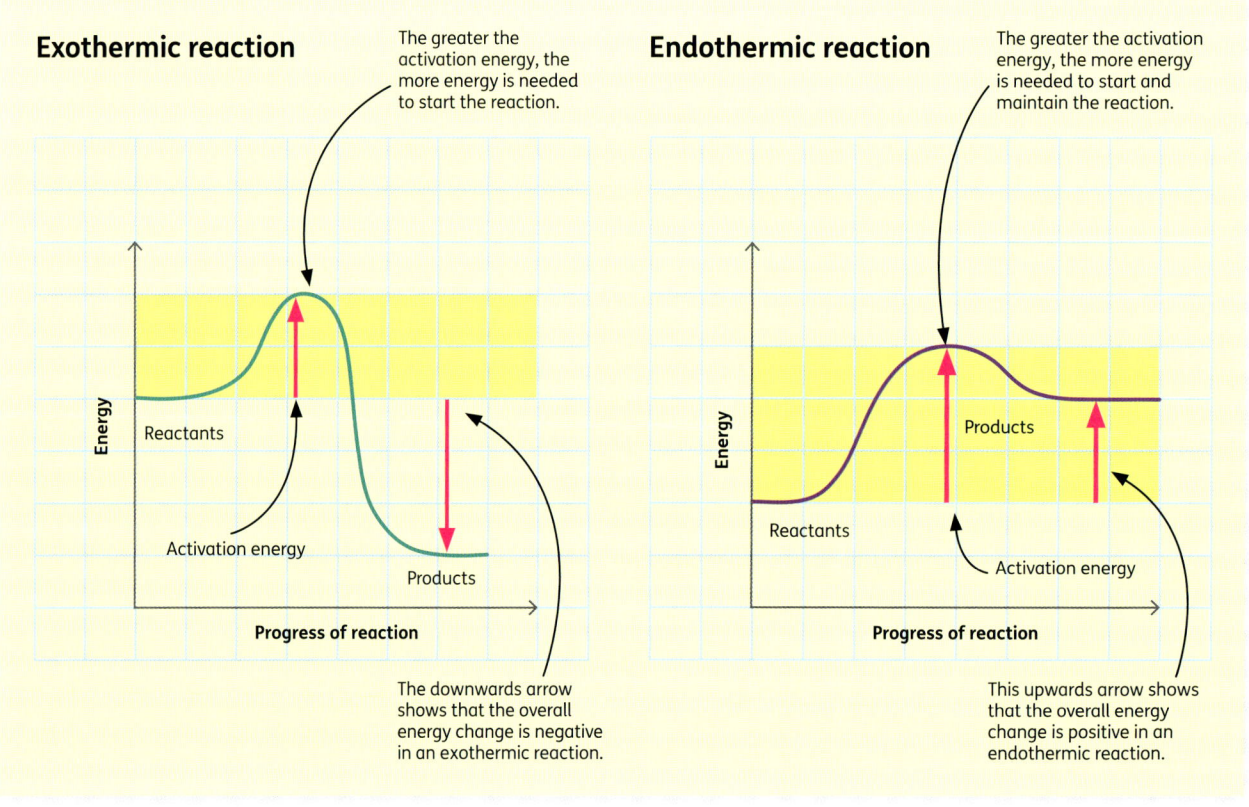

Calculating Energy Changes

Key facts

- Bond energies are the amounts of energy required to break one mole of chemical bonds.
- The energy change associated with a reaction is determined by subtracting the bond energies of the products from those of the reactants.
- For exothermic reactions, the energy change is negative, whereas for endothermic reactions, it is positive.

Bond energies

Energy is required to break chemical bonds and is released when bonds form. The energy involved in these processes is referred to as **bond energy**. The energy change in a reaction can be determined by calculating the bond energies of the bonds present in the reactants and products. Bond energies are measured in **kilojoules per mole** of bonds broken. Higher bond energies indicate stronger bonds.

bond energies of reactants − bond energies of products = energy change

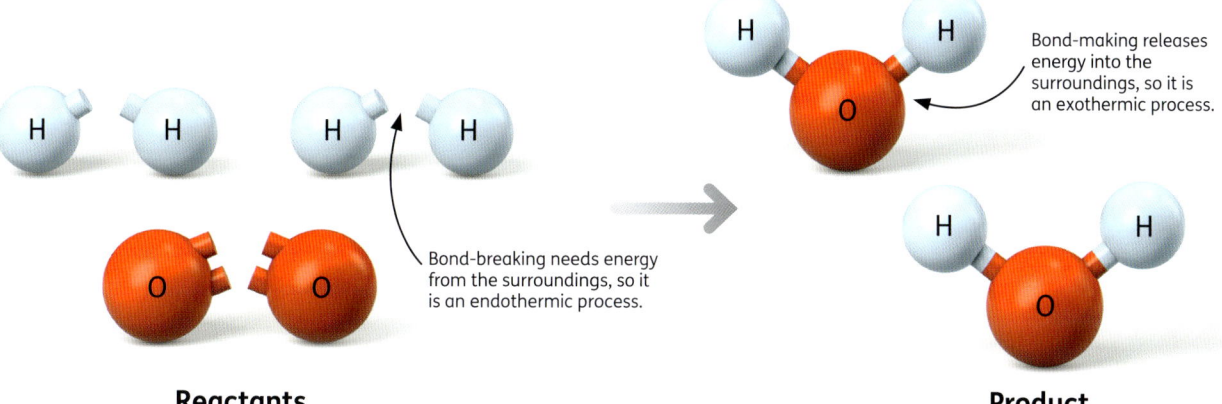

Reactants → Product

Bond-breaking needs energy from the surroundings, so it is an endothermic process.

Bond-making releases energy into the surroundings, so it is an exothermic process.

Science skills

You need to be able to calculate the energy in a reaction. The reaction between oxygen and hydrogen above will be the one used to explain how to carry out this calculation. You will be provided with bond energies in your exam so there is no need to remember these values. The equation for the reaction is: $2H_2 + O_2 \rightarrow 2H_2O$

1. Identify bonds to be broken from an equation or diagram:	2. Identify bonds to be formed from an equation or diagram:	3. Energy change = bond energies of reactants − bond energies of products:
2 × (H–H) = 2 × 436 = 872 1 × (O=O) = 1 × 498 Total bond energy of reactants: 872 + 498 = 1370 kJ/mol	4 × (O–H) = 4 × 463 = 1852 Total bond energy of products: 1852 kJ/mol	1370 − 1852 = −482 kJ/mol The negative value indicates the reaction is exothermic.

Energy Changes 47

Energy Changes

Chemical Cells

> ### Key facts
> - A battery has one or more voltaic cells.
> - Non-rechargeable batteries lose their chemicals and require replacement.
> - Rechargeable batteries can be recharged by reversing the reaction with an external power source.
> - A larger voltage is produced when there is a greater difference in metal reactivity.

A simple **voltaic cell** is a device that generates electrical energy from chemical reactions. It is made by placing two different metals in an electrolyte solution.

Batteries

A **battery** contains one or more voltaic cells that convert chemical energy into electrical energy. It usually has a metal or plastic casing and two terminals for circuit connection. Alkaline batteries power devices like torches, toys and remote controls, and can be single-use or rechargeable.

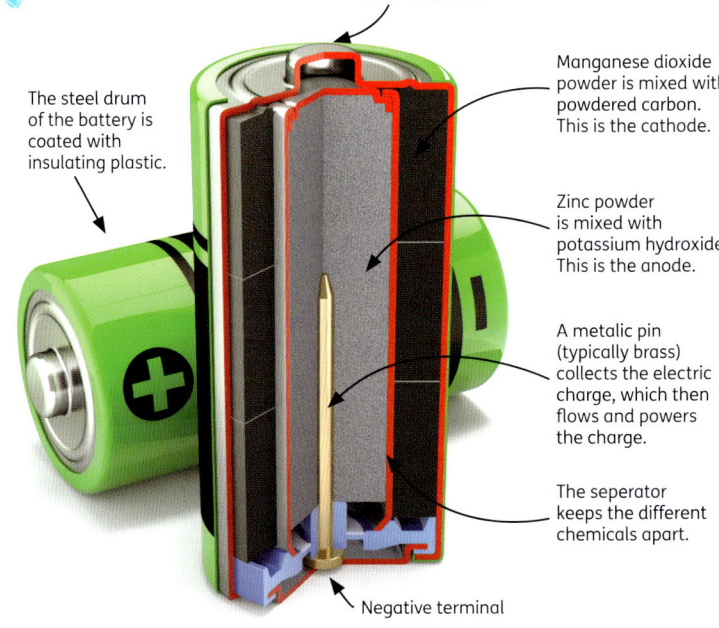

- Positive terminal
- The steel drum of the battery is coated with insulating plastic.
- Manganese dioxide powder is mixed with powdered carbon. This is the cathode.
- Zinc powder is mixed with potassium hydroxide. This is the anode.
- A metalic pin (typically brass) collects the electric charge, which then flows and powers the charge.
- The seperator keeps the different chemicals apart.
- Negative terminal

How voltaic cells work

Voltaic cells generate energy through chemical reactions that **transfer electrons**. At one terminal, electrons are released; at the other, they are gained. This creates a flow of electrons in the circuit.

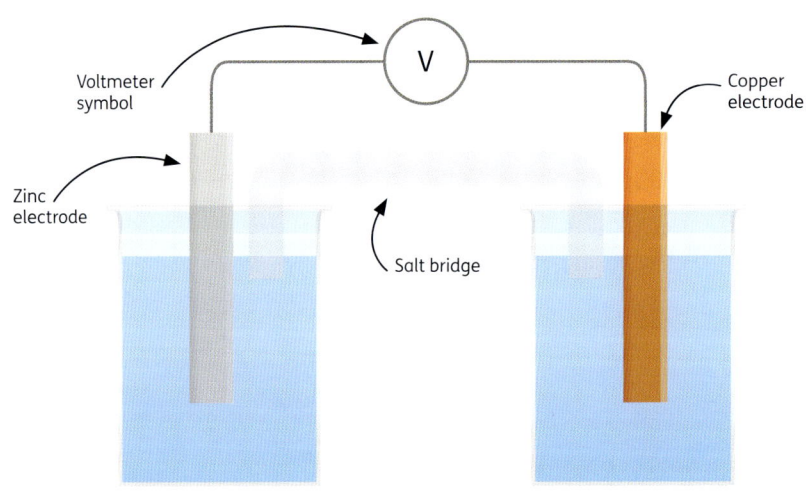

Zinc is more reactive than copper, which means it gives up its electrons more readily. Zinc becomes the negative terminal of the cell.

Copper metal is less reactive than zinc, therefore copper ions tend to gain electrons. The copper becomes the positive terminal.

Energy Changes

Fuel Cells

Key facts

- A fuel undergoes oxidation through an electrochemical reaction with oxygen (or air).
- In a hydrogen–oxygen fuel cell, hydrogen reacts with oxygen to form water.
- Hydrogen loses electrons, undergoing oxidation to form hydrogen ions.
- Oxygen interacts with hydrogen ions and electrons, subsequently being reduced to water.
- The reaction generates a potential difference, resulting in an electric current.

How does a fuel cell work?

Within a hydrogen–oxygen fuel cell, the oxidation of hydrogen occurs at the anode (negative electrode), resulting in the production of hydrogen ions and electrons. The hydrogen ions travel through a membrane to reach the cathode (positive electrode) while the electrons are directed there via an external circuit. At the cathode, oxygen undergoes a reduction reaction with hydrogen ions and electrons to form water.

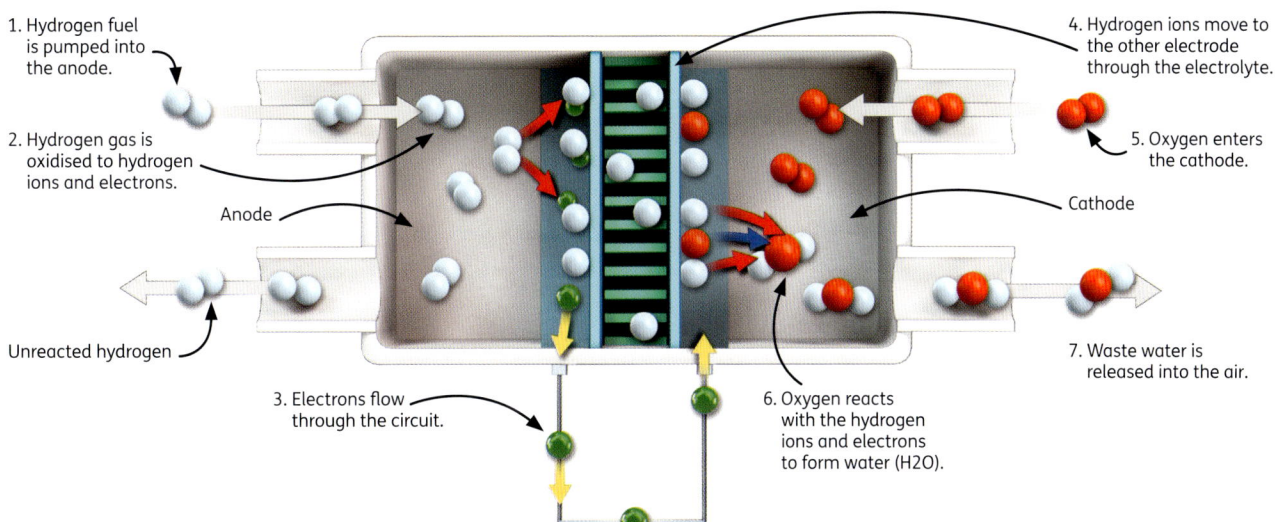

1. Hydrogen fuel is pumped into the anode.
2. Hydrogen gas is oxidised to hydrogen ions and electrons.
3. Electrons flow through the circuit.
4. Hydrogen ions move to the other electrode through the electrolyte.
5. Oxygen enters the cathode.
6. Oxygen reacts with the hydrogen ions and electrons to form water (H_2O).
7. Waste water is released into the air.

Unreacted hydrogen • Anode • Cathode

Comparing batteries and fuel cells

Fuel cells and batteries both use electrochemical reactions to generate a potential difference. However, fuel cells require a fuel source, unlike batteries. They also have other differences.

Feature	Batteries	Fuel cells
Energy storage	Stores chemical energy	Generates electrical energy from fuel
Fuel source	No external fuel needed	Requires continuous fuel supply (e.g. hydrogen)
Emissions	None	Water (if hydrogen is used)
Recharge	Rechargeable via electrical input	Continuous operation with fuel
Efficiency	Generally, less efficient due to energy conversion losses	Higher efficiency due to direct conversion
Application	Common in portable devices and electric vehicles	Used in applications requiring high efficiency and clean energy, such as spacecraft and some vehicles

Brain Booster

Energy Changes Recap Quiz

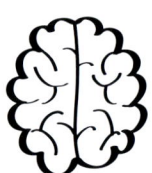

 Find a pen and paper and work through these revision questions.

1. State the definition of an exothermic reaction.
2. List **three** examples of exothermic reactions.
3. Identify the main feature of an endothermic reaction.
4. Describe a reaction profile for an exothermic reaction.
5. Describe a reaction profile for an endothermic reaction.
6. Explain how bond energy can be calculated in a chemical reaction.
7. Explain how a hydrogen fuel cell works.
8. Describe what a voltaic cell is.
9. Which combination of metals would produce the largest voltage?
   copper–magnesium   copper–silver   iron–zinc
10. Evaluate the efficiency of fuel cells compared to batteries.
11. Calculate the bond energy change for the following reaction:
    $H_2 + Br_2 \rightarrow 2HBr$. The bond energies are as follows:
    H–H is 436 kJ/mol, Br–Br is 193 kJ/mol and H–Br is 366 kJ/mol.
12. Compare the features of batteries with fuel cells.

Check your answers on page **109**.

Rates of Reaction

At the end of this chapter, you should be able to:

- ✓ Define the rate of reaction and explain its importance in chemical processes.
- ✓ List methods to measure the rate of reaction including gas collection, mass loss and colour change.
- ✓ Describe collision theory and its role in determining the rate of reaction.
- ✓ Explain the concept of activation energy and its significance in chemical reactions.
- ✓ Identify factors that affect the rate of reaction, including concentration, temperature, surface area and catalysts.
- ✓ Understand the role of catalysts in increasing the rate of reaction.
- ✓ Explain the concept of reversible reactions.
- ✓ Define dynamic equilibrium and describe the conditions necessary for it to be established.
- ✓ Use Le Chatelier's principle to predict the effects of changes in concentration, temperature and pressure on equilibrium.

Rates of Reaction

Key facts

- The rate of a chemical reaction measures how quickly reactants are consumed or products form.
- Reactions vary in speed: rusting is slow, but explosions are rapid.
- Mean reaction rate is determined by dividing the quantity of reactant used or product formed by time.

Science skills

The mean rate of reaction can be calculated if both the quantity of reactant consumed or product formed and the time taken are known. The quantity may be expressed in terms of mass, volume or the number of moles of the substance.

$$\text{mean rate of reaction} = \frac{\text{quantity of reactant used or produced}}{\text{time taken}}$$

The **rate of a chemical reaction** measures how fast it occurs. It can be described by the speed at which reactants are used up or products are formed. The rate varies according to the reaction type and conditions. Different reactions occur at different rates.

Slow reactions

Slow reactions include:
- formation of crude oil
- formation of rust
- fermentation of sugars into alcohol.

Moderate reactions

Moderate reactions include:
- magnesium reacting with acid
- cooking food
- reaction of vinegar and baking soda.

Fast reactions
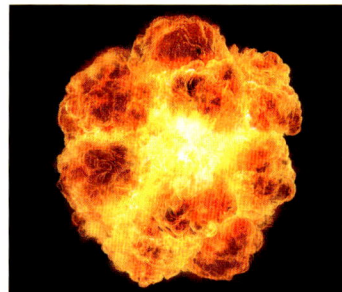
Fast reactions include:
- combustion of natural gas
- explosion of fireworks
- reaction of petrol in car engines.

Rate of reaction graphs

You are expected to be able to both draw and interpret a graph for rate of reaction. During a reaction, reactants decrease while products increase. A graph plotting quantity against time shows these changes. The gradient of the line represents the reaction rate.

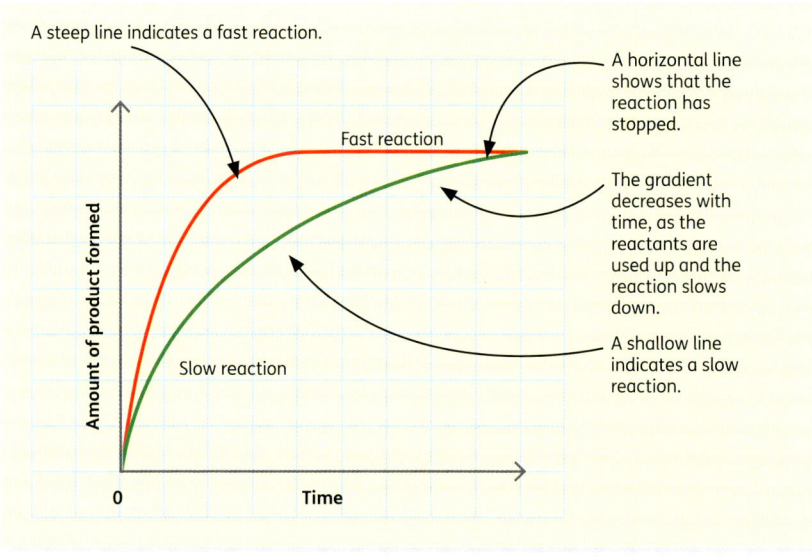

Measuring Rates of Reaction

Key facts

- Rates of reactions can be measured by recording the volume of gas produced, the loss or gain of mass over time or a colour change.
- The rate of reaction is determined by recording the mass of the reaction mixture and apparatus, and the time.

Exam tip

When confronted with an unfamiliar reaction, selecting the correct method requires a check of the equation. Look at the state symbols as this will lead you to the correct technique.

Rates of reaction and gas volume

A **gas syringe** measures **gas** volumes accurately, typically in 100 cm³ increments of 1 cm³. It is more convenient than an upturned measuring cylinder in water. To determine the rate of reaction, record the gas volume produced over time. The gradient of a volume versus time graph indicates the reaction rate.

Rates of reaction and mass

In the laboratory, a **top pan balance** can be used to measure mass. For example, a dense gas like carbon dioxide can be measured by its loss from a reaction mixture. The total mass of reactants and products remains constant, but the reaction mixture loses mass as the gas escapes into the surroundings.

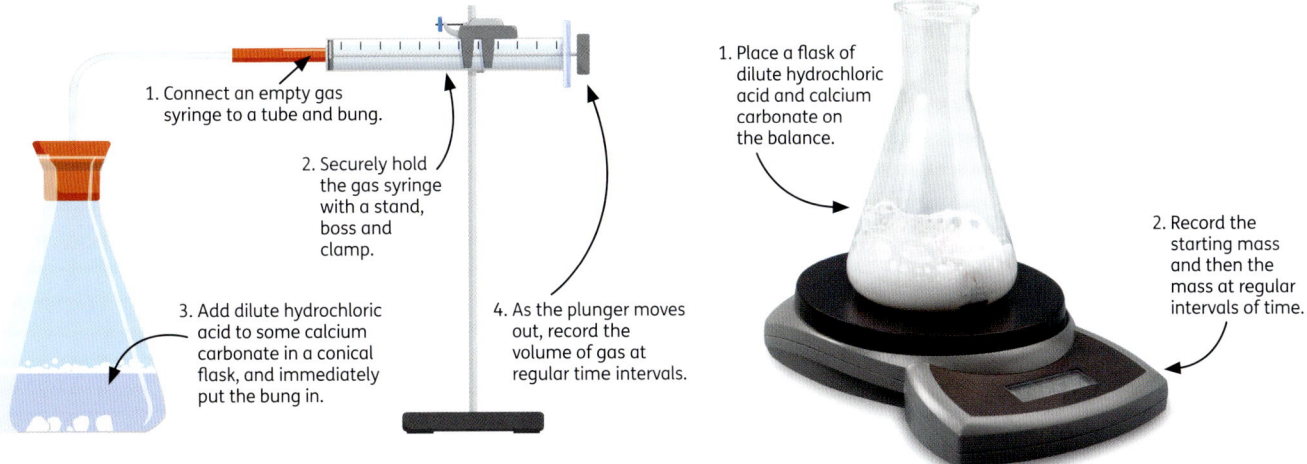

1. Connect an empty gas syringe to a tube and bung.
2. Securely hold the gas syringe with a stand, boss and clamp.
3. Add dilute hydrochloric acid to some calcium carbonate in a conical flask, and immediately put the bung in.
4. As the plunger moves out, record the volume of gas at regular time intervals.

1. Place a flask of dilute hydrochloric acid and calcium carbonate on the balance.
2. Record the starting mass and then the mass at regular intervals of time.

Rates of reaction and colour change

A **precipitate** is an insoluble substance formed when two solutions react, making the mixture **cloudy**. You can measure the reaction rate by timing how long it takes to get too cloudy to see through – the longer this takes, the slower the rate of reaction.

1. Draw a cross on a piece of paper. Place a beaker or flask of sodium thiosulfate solution on the paper.

2. Add dilute hydrochloric acid and start the stopwatch. The reaction mixture begins to turn cloudy.

3. Keep looking through the liquid. Stop timing when the cross just disappears from sight. Record the reading to the nearest whole second.

Rates of Reaction

Collision Theory

Collision theory describes chemical reactions and their rates. For a chemical reaction to occur between two substances, their particles must collide with **sufficient energy**. The more **successful collisions**, the faster the reaction.

Reaction rates and catalysts

A catalyst increases the speed of a chemical reaction without being used up. After the reaction, the catalyst remains unchanged and can be reused. Using a catalyst results in a lower activation energy being required for the reaction. Enzymes serve as biological catalysts. Different reactions need different catalysts.

The activation energy is defined as the minimum energy needed for a reaction to take place. Catalysts offer an alternative reaction pathway with lower activation energy. By reducing the energy necessary for collisions, they increase the rate of successful collisions.

Key facts

- Chemical reactions only occur when the reactant particles collide with sufficient energy.
- The higher the frequency of successful collisions, the faster the rate of reaction.
- Reacting particles in chemical reactions may include atoms, ions or molecules.
- Reaction rates can be altered by changing the temperature, pressure, concentration or surface area, or by adding a catalyst.

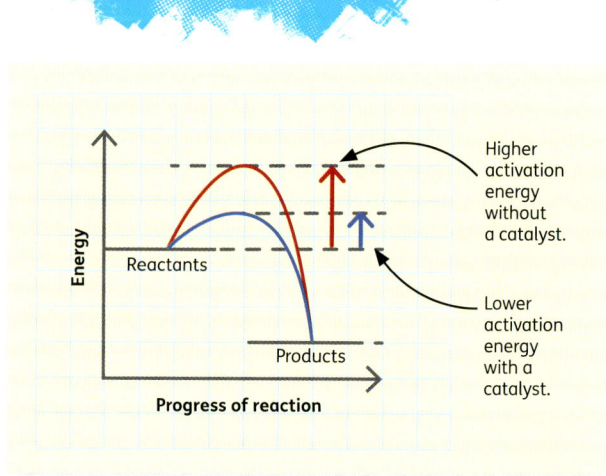

An unsuccessful collision

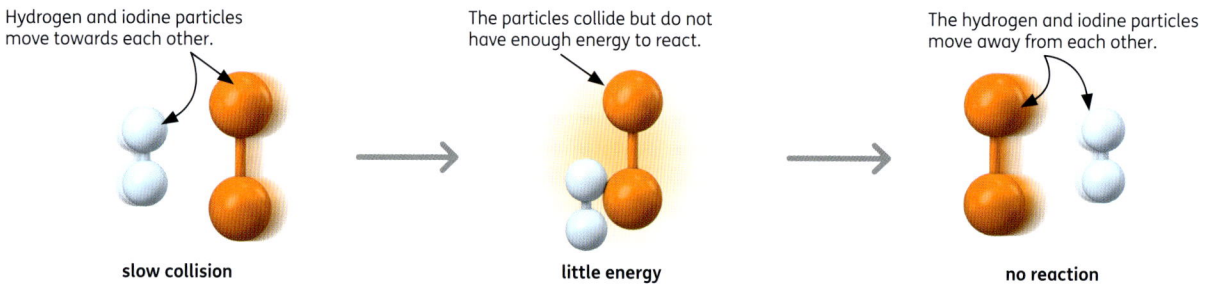

Hydrogen and iodine particles move towards each other. | The particles collide but do not have enough energy to react. | The hydrogen and iodine particles move away from each other.

slow collision — little energy — no reaction

A successful collision

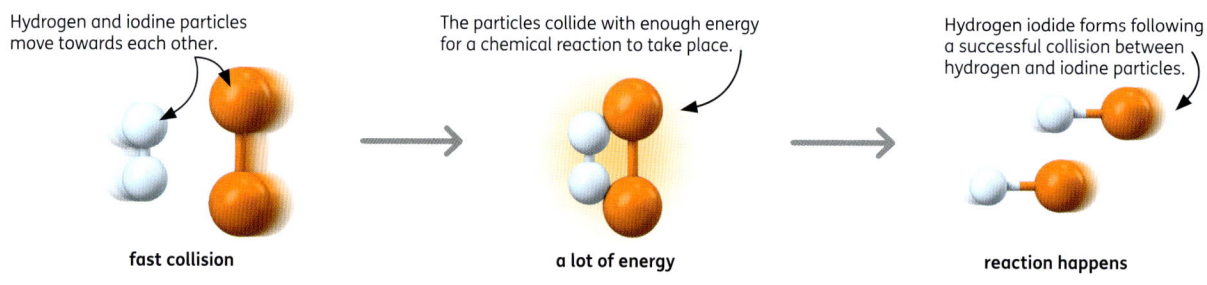

Hydrogen and iodine particles move towards each other. | The particles collide with enough energy for a chemical reaction to take place. | Hydrogen iodide forms following a successful collision between hydrogen and iodine particles.

fast collision — a lot of energy — reaction happens

Rates of Reaction

Reaction rates and temperature

Higher temperatures increase reaction rates because the particles move faster and collide more often, leading to a greater number of successful collisions.

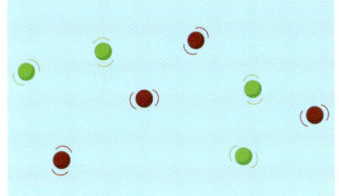

Low temperature and low reaction rate
Infrequent collisions with only a small proportion that are successful.

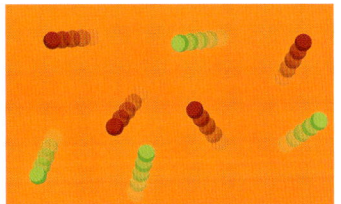

High temperature and high reaction rate
More frequent collisions and with a high proportion that are successful.

Reaction rates and concentration or pressure

Higher reactant concentration in solution increases the reaction rate due to more frequent collisions. Likewise, increasing gas pressure leads to more particle collisions.

Low concentration or low pressure
Particles are not crowded so they do not collide often.

High concentration or high pressure
Particles are more crowded so they collide more often.

Reaction rates and surface area

Increasing the surface area of a solid reactant results in a higher reaction rate. Smaller pieces have a larger surface area to volume ratio for the same mass of reactant. This exposes more particles on the surface and leads to more frequent collisions.

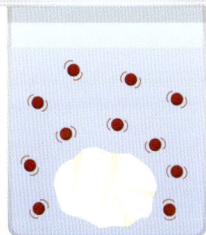

Large lumps
Low rates of collisions so low rates of reaction.

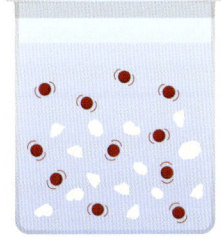

Small lumps
High rates of collisions so high rates of reaction.

RAPPING UP!

Here's the topic I'm rapping.
Lets start on the left, on this side are **reactants**.
When atoms collide, we have a reaction.
To increase the rate,
we can make some adaptions.

If **temperature's** low,
then its slow they be acting.
Increase the temp –
now they moving with passion.

The same goes for pressure,
when high they be packed in,
not the same for when
concentration is lacking.

Turn it to dust and it speeds the rate up.
Chuck in a **catalyst** just for good luck.
For rates of reaction we learn the above
don't like my raps I don't give a …

Final thing now, I'll be quick as a flash.
Collision theory's when particles clash'
With enough energy they can react
a product is formed, now we call that a wrap.

Rates of Reaction

Reversible Reactions

Key facts

- A reversible reaction includes both a forward reaction and a reverse reaction.
- The symbol ⇌ indicates a reversible reaction.

Science skills

Reversible reaction equations use a symbol (⇌) to indicate that the reaction can proceed in either direction, allowing products to react and form reactants again.

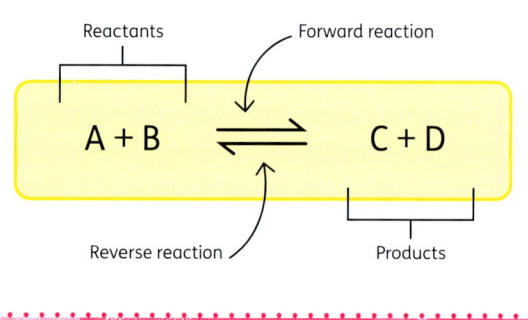

Some chemical reactions are reversible. These reactions can be reversed by altering reaction conditions, such as temperature, pressure and concentration.

Reversible reaction example

Hydrated copper sulfate is blue. When heated, the water is removed from the hydrated form leaving white anhydrous copper sulfate. The dot in the hydrated copper sulfate formula indicates the ratio of water molecules that are attached to the copper sulfate.

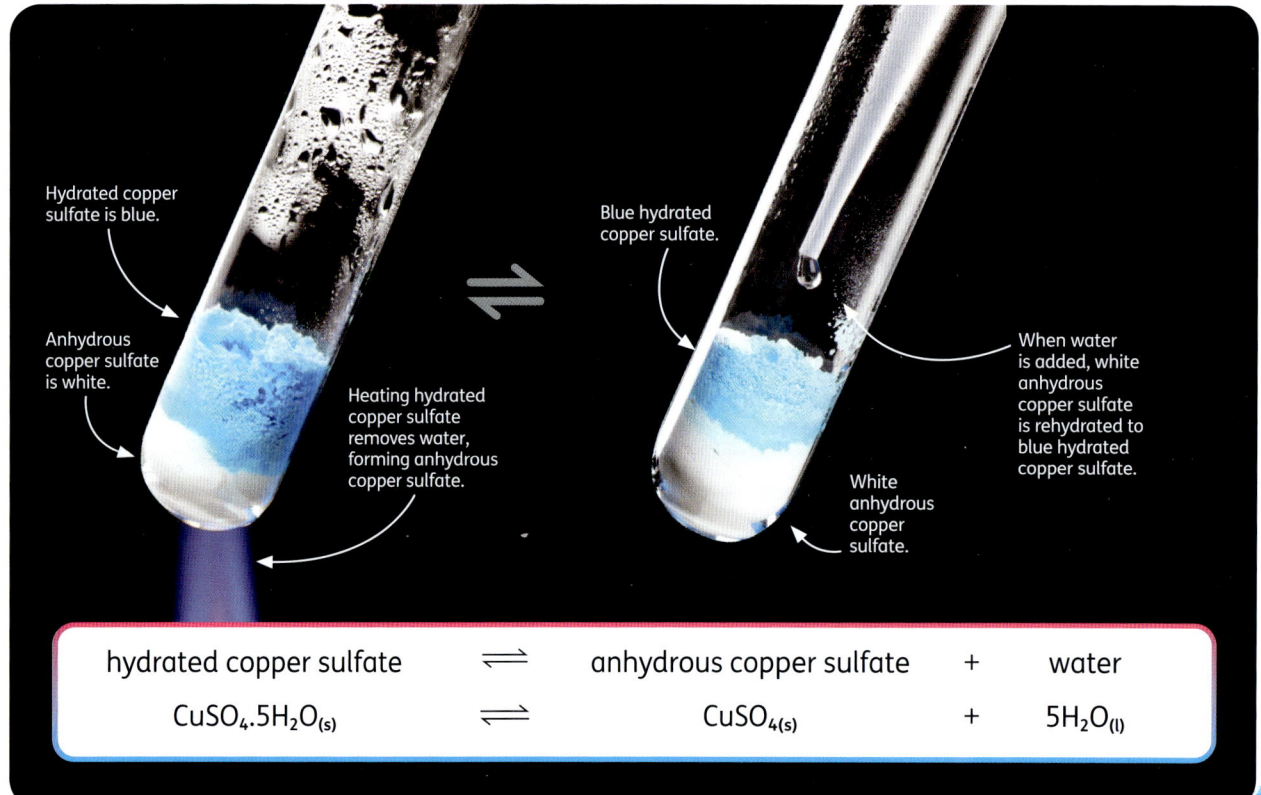

hydrated copper sulfate ⇌ anhydrous copper sulfate + water
$CuSO_4 \cdot 5H_2O_{(s)}$ ⇌ $CuSO_{4(s)}$ + $5H_2O_{(l)}$

Equilibrium

> **Key facts**
>
> - Reversible reactions in closed systems reach equilibrium when the rates of forward and reverse reactions are equal.
> - At equilibrium, reactant and product concentrations remain constant.

In a **closed system**, a reversible reaction reaches **equilibrium**, where the forward and reverse reactions occur at equal rates. This results in constant concentrations of reactants and products, although these concentrations may not be equal.

Dynamic equilibrium

Equilibrium occurs when the forward and reverse reactions proceed at the same rate. The position of equilibrium indicates the concentration at equilibrium. When the equilibrium shifts to the right, there are more products than reactants; when it shifts to the left, there are more reactants than products.

The term "dynamic equilibrium" is used as a reminder that, even though the concentrations of reactants and products remain constant, the molecules are continuously reacting. This ongoing and balanced process means that reactants are turning into products and products are turning into reactants at the same rate, making the equilibrium dynamic rather than static.

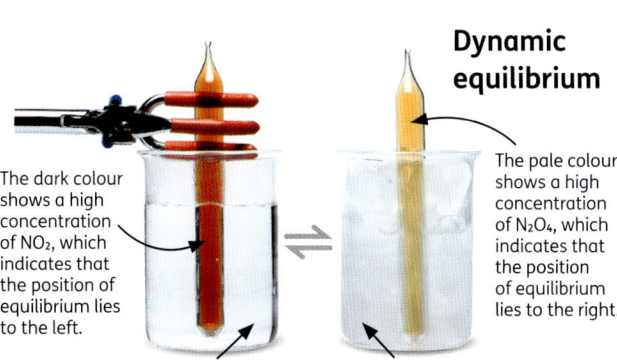

Dynamic equilibrium

The dark colour shows a high concentration of NO_2, which indicates that the position of equilibrium lies to the left. — Hot water

The pale colour shows a high concentration of N_2O_4, which indicates that the position of equilibrium lies to the right. — Cold water

Rates of Reaction

RAPPING UP!

I'll start this in a place that's easy: you all know **chemicals** react. This next part – better believe me – most go forward but some'll go back.

We call these **reversible** reactions. This is the symbol that shows if heat goes out when these chemicals reacting. Heat goes in when they **decompose**.

Sometimes they can happen at once – at the same rate – that's **equilibrium**.

More to this word, so I need you to listen: this only happens if in a closed system. That means it's **sealed**, if you're ever in doubt; nothing gets in and then nothing gets out.

Although equal's in this word, their amounts aren't always alike. If concentration of products is **higher**, then equilibrium lies to the right.

If concentration of products is lower, then equilibrium lies to the left. There is one more thing that I'd like to show ya: **Le Chatelier's principle** – say it with chest.

If you change a **condition**, the system will shift to counter the change. This moves equilibrium position to keep all the following factors the same:

concentration – temperature – pressure. Gotta go now; I'll leave you this fact: if the forward reaction gives out heat, raising the **temperature** makes it go back.

Brain Booster

Rates of Reaction Recap Quiz

 Find a pen and paper and work through these revision questions.

1. What is the definition of the rate of a reaction?
2. Describe **two** methods for measuring the rate of a reaction.
3. Explain the concept of collision theory in chemical reactions.
4. How does temperature affect the rate of a chemical reaction?
5. Explain how concentration can affect the rate of reaction.
6. How does surface area influence the rate of reaction?
7. What is the effect of a catalyst on the rate of a reaction?
8. Define a reversible reaction.
9. Use the example of hydrated copper sulfate to explain a reversible reaction.
10. What is the symbol used in reversible reactions?
11. What is dynamic equilibrium?
12. Explain the concept of activation energy in collision theory.

Check your answers on pages **109–110**.

Organic Chemistry

At the end of this chapter, you should be able to:

- ✓ Identify and name different organic compounds.
- ✓ Draw and describe the structure and properties of alkanes and alkenes.
- ✓ Describe the process of cracking and why it is needed.
- ✓ Explain how fractional distillation is used to separate crude oil.
- ✓ Explain the functional groups and their reactions.
- ✓ Explain how an ester is formed from an alcohol and a carboxylic acid.
- ✓ Compare and contrast addition polymerisation and condensation polymerisation.
- ✓ Describe the structure of DNA and other naturally occurring polymers.

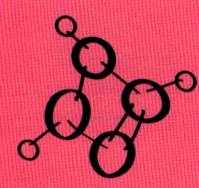

Organic Chemistry

Crude Oil and Hydrocarbons

Key facts

- Crude oil is a fossil fuel and mainly composed of hydrocarbon molecules.
- Hydrocarbons are compounds made of hydrogen and carbon atoms only.
- Most hydrocarbons in crude oil are alkanes.
- Alkanes are saturated hydrocarbons.

Crude oil

Many hundreds of millions of years ago the oceans were full of tiny, microscopic creatures known as **plankton**. When these plankton died, they sank down to the ocean floor, becoming part of a rich, organic sludge. Over time, layer upon layer of mud and silt buried this organic material deeper and deeper. Over many millions of years, pressure and temperatures rose, causing the plankton sludge to turn into **crude oil**.

Crude oil is a thick gloopy liquid made up of a huge number of compounds. Most of these compounds are hydrocarbons called **alkanes**. Crude oil is known as a **finite** resource. This is what we call a natural resource that cannot be replaced as quickly as it is used.

The properties of **hydrocarbons**, such as boiling point, viscosity and flammability, change with molecular size, influencing their use as fuels.

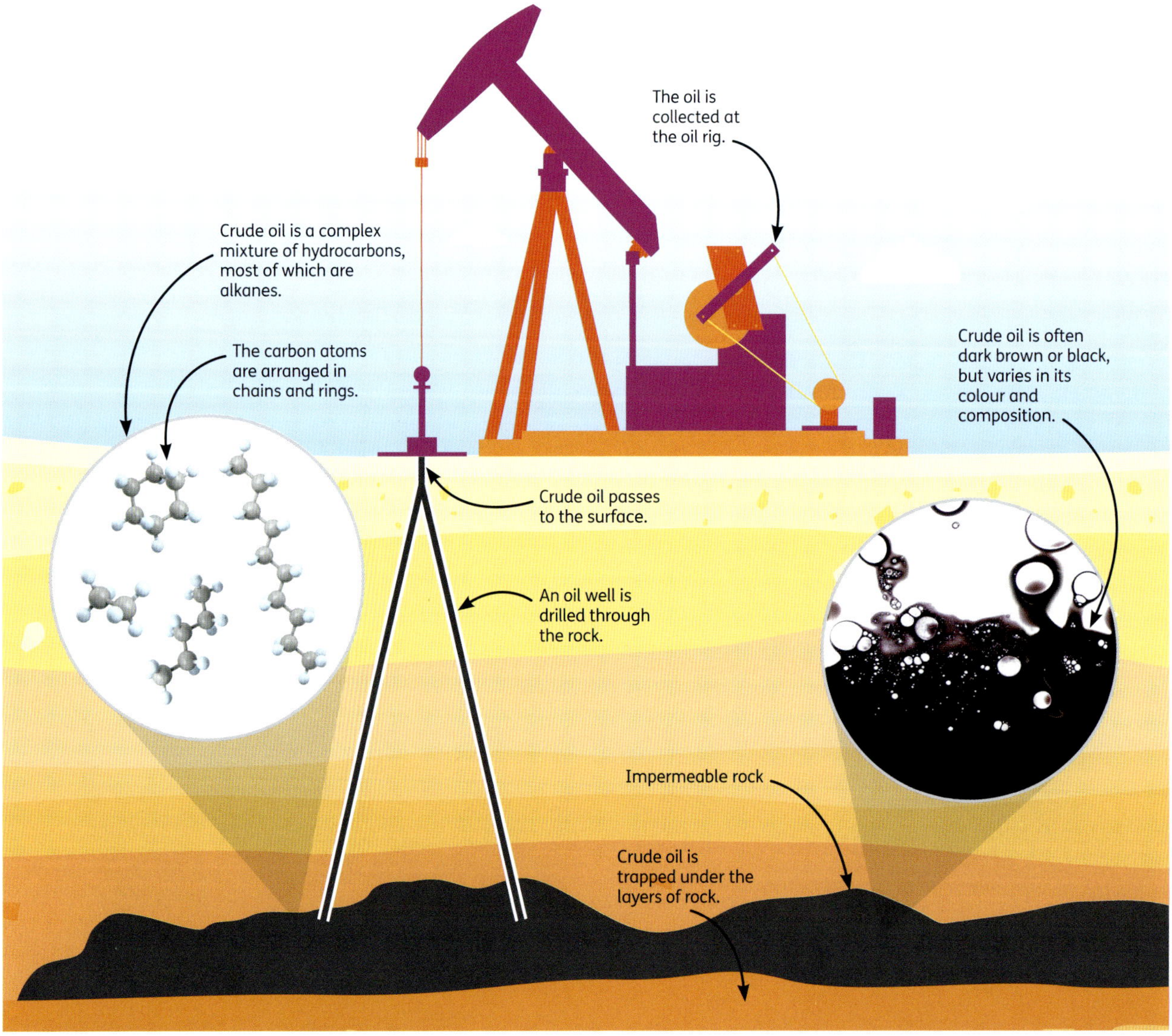

- The oil is collected at the oil rig.
- Crude oil is a complex mixture of hydrocarbons, most of which are alkanes.
- The carbon atoms are arranged in chains and rings.
- Crude oil is often dark brown or black, but varies in its colour and composition.
- Crude oil passes to the surface.
- An oil well is drilled through the rock.
- Impermeable rock
- Crude oil is trapped under the layers of rock.

Organic Chemistry

RAPPING UP!

Methane, ethane and propane, butane,
those are the first four alkanes. Alkanes
These are the things they contain
carbon and **HY-dro gen** own-lay,
here's how arranged.

Look at the chains.
It all starts with methane.
Burns with the cleanest flame.
C_nH_{2n} plus twain.

General formula. Clock it.
Double the number of **hydrogens** on it.
Add 2 extra here now you got it.
Ethane's next for this topic.

Follow the general **formula** for it.
That's now got one more carbon in this.
That means its now C_2H_6.

Alkanes

The general formula for the homologous series of **alkanes** is C_nH_{2n+2}. We call families of compounds homologous if they possess the same **functional group** and similar chemical properties. A functional group is what we call a group of atoms that give a molecule its characteristic chemical properties. Alkanes only contain single carbon–carbon covalent bonds. Alkanes are referred to as **saturated hydrocarbons** because each molecule contains the maximum number of hydrogen atoms possible. For more on alkenes, see pages 64–66.

	Formula	Structural formula	Displayed formula
Methane	CH_4	CH_4	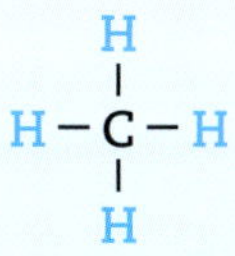 H–C(H,H)–H
Ethane	C_2H_6	CH_3CH_3	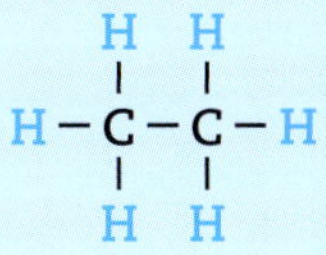 H–C(H,H)–C(H,H)–H
Propane	C_3H_8	$CH_3CH_2CH_3$	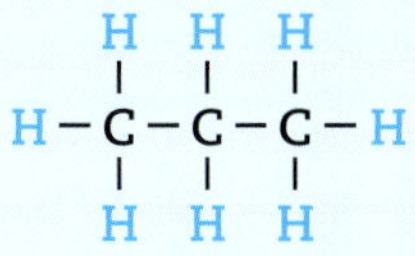 H–C(H,H)–C(H,H)–C(H,H)–H
Butane	C_4H_{10}	$CH_3CH_2CH_2CH_3$	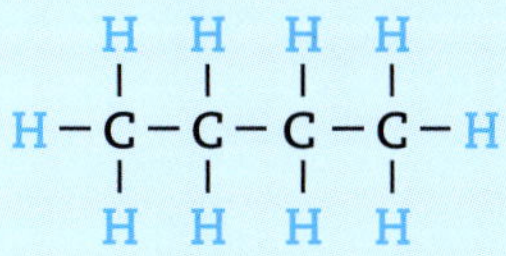 H–C(H,H)–C(H,H)–C(H,H)–C(H,H)–H

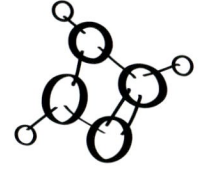

Organic Chemistry

Fractional Distillation

RAPPING UP!

There are three main **fuels** we use in life,
but right now, all I wanna talk about's this one.

What do you mean which one?
Crude oil's up in this system.
Each fraction has its conditions.
Each fraction has its own uses.
Learn each one, no excuses.
Energy's what it **produces**.

Let me explain what this juice is –
it's not useless.
It's a mix of **hydrocarbons**
formed from hydrogen and carbon.
Now, most of them are liquids,
but some are solids when they harden.
You gonna have to beg my pardon,
I had to advertise a bargain.
Now the temp up top is coolest,
but down here is fire – call it arson.

Bitumen's the bottom;
we got the petrol at the top;
we got kerosene up in the middle;
diesel's so easily forgot.

Methane gas just can't be stopped,
its boiling point just ain't a lot.
That's why it comes out of the top right here
not the bottom where it's hot.

Key facts

- Crude oil is separated into fractions by heating it and using fractional distillation.
- Different hydrocarbons in crude oil have varying boiling points.

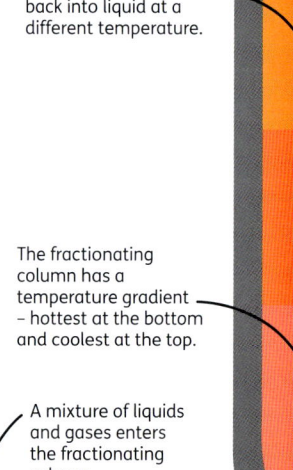

Substances that are gases at room temperature collect at the top of the column.

The higher up the column, the runnier and easier to ignite the fractions become.

The vapour cools as it rises, with each substance condensing back into liquid at a different temperature.

The fractionating column has a temperature gradient – hottest at the bottom and coolest at the top.

Crude oil

Crude oil is heated strongly in an industrial oil refinery.

A mixture of liquids and gases enters the fractionating column.

Organic Chemistry

Properties of fractions

The properties of different fractions in crude oil vary. You should be able to predict the properties of a crude oil fraction, either from where it condenses in the fractionating column or from the length of the hydrocarbon chain.

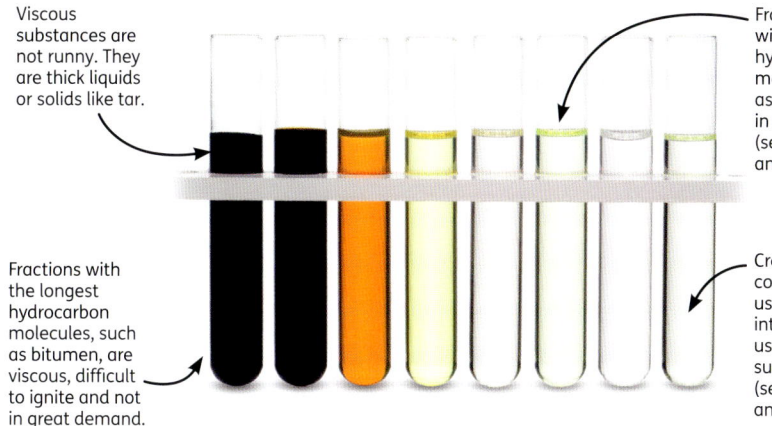

Viscous substances are not runny. They are thick liquids or solids like tar.

Fractions with the longest hydrocarbon molecules, such as bitumen, are viscous, difficult to ignite and not in great demand.

Fractions with shorter hydrocarbon molecules, such as fuel oil, are in high demand (see pages 64 and 65).

Cracking converts less useful fractions into more useful fractions, such as petrol (see pages 64 and 65).

1–4 carbon atoms
Highly flammable gases

Refinery gases
Heating and cooking

4–12 carbon atoms
Highly flammable liquids with very low viscosity

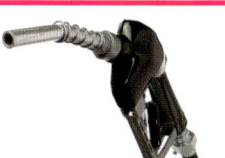

Petrol
Fuel for cars

7–14 carbon atoms
Very flammable liquids with low viscosity

Naphtha
Feedstock for the petrochemical industry

11–15 carbon atoms
Flammable liquids with low viscosity

Kerosene
Fuel for aircraft

14–19 carbon atoms
Flammable but viscous liquids

Diesel oil
Fuel for some trains and cars

18–30 carbon atoms
Very viscous liquids, difficult to ignite

Fuel oil
Fuel for large ships and some power stations

30+ carbon atoms
Solids at room temperature

Bitumen
Waterproofing roofs and surfacing roads

Organic Chemistry

Cracking and Alkenes

Supply and demand

The majority of hydrocarbons extracted from crude oil through fractional distillation are the heavier, long-chain compounds rather than the lighter varieties. However, it is the lighter hydrocarbons that are more desirable for use as fuels due to their ease of ignition and clean combustion. To make these hydrocarbons more useful, the process of **cracking** is used. This involves breaking down these larger molecules into smaller, more valuable hydrocarbons, such as petrol and ethene, which are in higher demand.

Key facts

- Cracking is the process of breaking down less useful long-chain hydrocarbons into smaller, more useful shorter-chain hydrocarbons.
- Cracking is a thermal decomposition reaction.
- Cracking requires a catalyst and a high temperature.
- Alkenes are hydrocarbons with a carbon–carbon double bond, making them more reactive than alkanes.
- The general formula for alkenes is C_nH_{2n}.

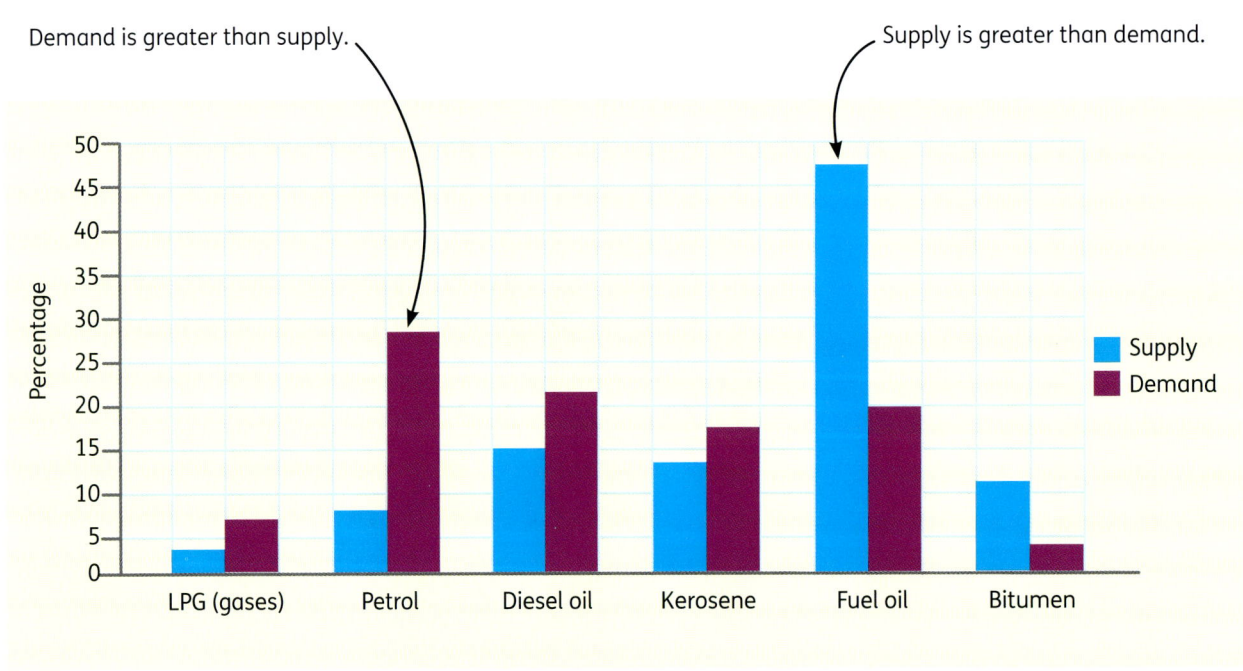

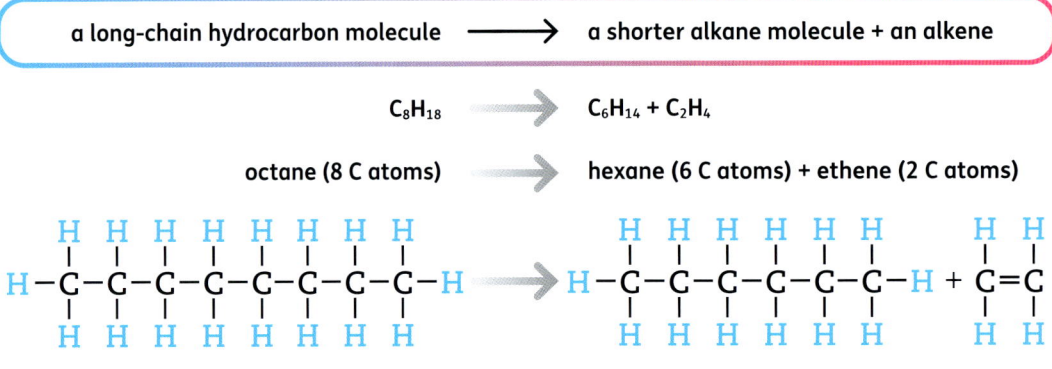

Organic Chemistry 65

Cracking

Cracking is achieved through thermal decomposition, meaning the process uses heat to break chemical bonds. There are two main types of cracking: **catalytic cracking** and **steam cracking**. Catalytic cracking uses a heated catalyst to break down the hydrocarbons, while steam cracking uses extremely high temperatures and steam to achieve the same result.

The smaller hydrocarbons produced in cracking are more useful because they are more volatile and burn more cleanly, making them ideal for fuels and as feedstock for the petrochemical industry.

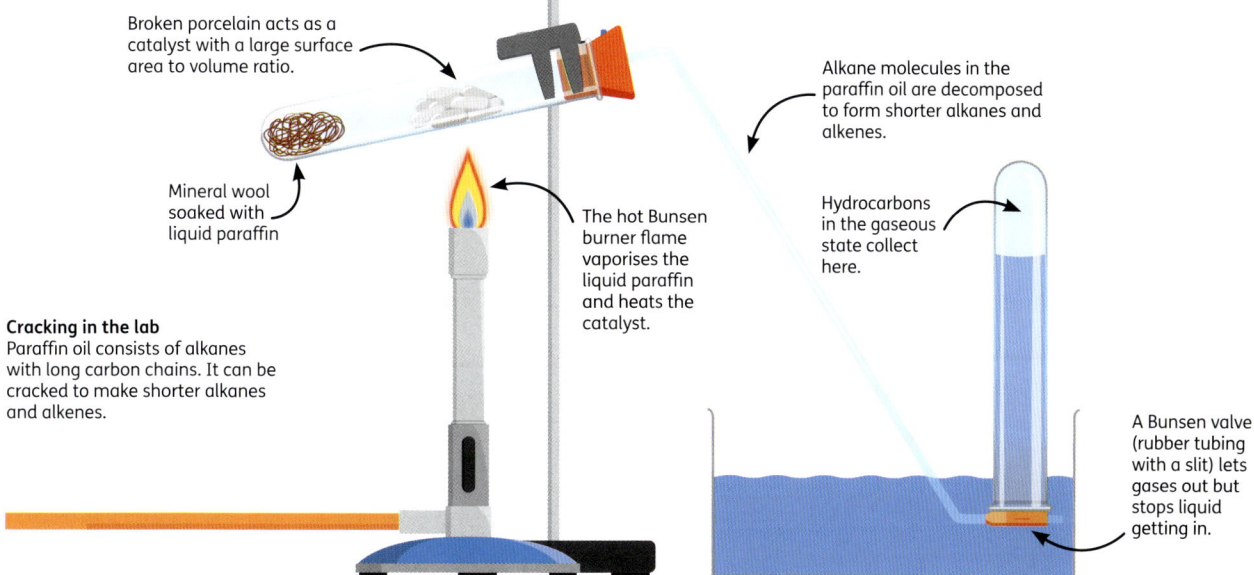

Broken porcelain acts as a catalyst with a large surface area to volume ratio.

Alkane molecules in the paraffin oil are decomposed to form shorter alkanes and alkenes.

Mineral wool soaked with liquid paraffin

The hot Bunsen burner flame vaporises the liquid paraffin and heats the catalyst.

Hydrocarbons in the gaseous state collect here.

Cracking in the lab
Paraffin oil consists of alkanes with long carbon chains. It can be cracked to make shorter alkanes and alkenes.

A Bunsen valve (rubber tubing with a slit) lets gases out but stops liquid getting in.

Alkenes

During the cracking process, some of the smaller molecules produced are hydrocarbons that contain a carbon–carbon double bond (C=C) in their structure. These molecules are known as **alkenes** and conform to the general formula C_nH_{2n}. Alkenes are classified as **unsaturated hydrocarbons** due to the presence of the **double bond**, resulting in fewer hydrogen atoms compared to an alkane with the same number of carbon atoms. (See also the rap on page 61.)

	Formula	Structural formula	Displayed formula
Ethene	C_2H_4	$CH_2{=}CH_2$	H₂C=CH₂ (displayed)
Propene	C_3H_6	$CH_3CH{=}CH_2$	H–C–C=C (displayed)
Butene	C_4H_8	$CH_3CH_2CH{=}CH_2$	H–C–C–C=C (displayed)
Pentene	C_5H_{10}	$CH_3CH_2CH_2CH{=}CH_2$	H–C–C–C–C=C (displayed)

Organic Chemistry

Reactions of Alkenes

Key facts

- Alkenes undergo addition reactions due to their C=C bond.
- One product is produced when an addition reaction occurs.
- Addition with hydrogen generates alkanes; addition with halogens produces halogenoalkanes.
- Bromine water changes colour from orange to colourless when it reacts with an alkene.
- In contrast, bromine water remains orange when it is mixed with an alkane.

Addition reactions

In an addition reaction, two substances combine to create a single product. Alkenes possess a carbon–carbon double bond (C=C), enabling them to participate in addition reactions. Specifically, alkenes react with hydrogen to produce alkanes and with bromine to generate dibromo compounds. Alkenes can also polymerise through addition reactions to form addition polymers.

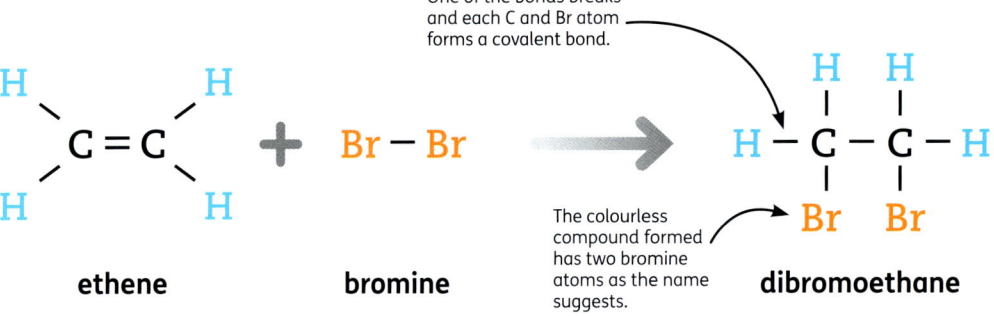

ethene + bromine → dibromoethane

One of the bonds breaks and each C and Br atom forms a covalent bond.

The colourless compound formed has two bromine atoms as the name suggests.

Testing for alkenes

Bromine water is used to detect the presence of alkenes (unsaturated hydrocarbons). Bromine water changes from orange to colourless when added to alkenes, but when added to alkanes, bromine water stays orange-brown. This reaction is classified as an addition reaction.

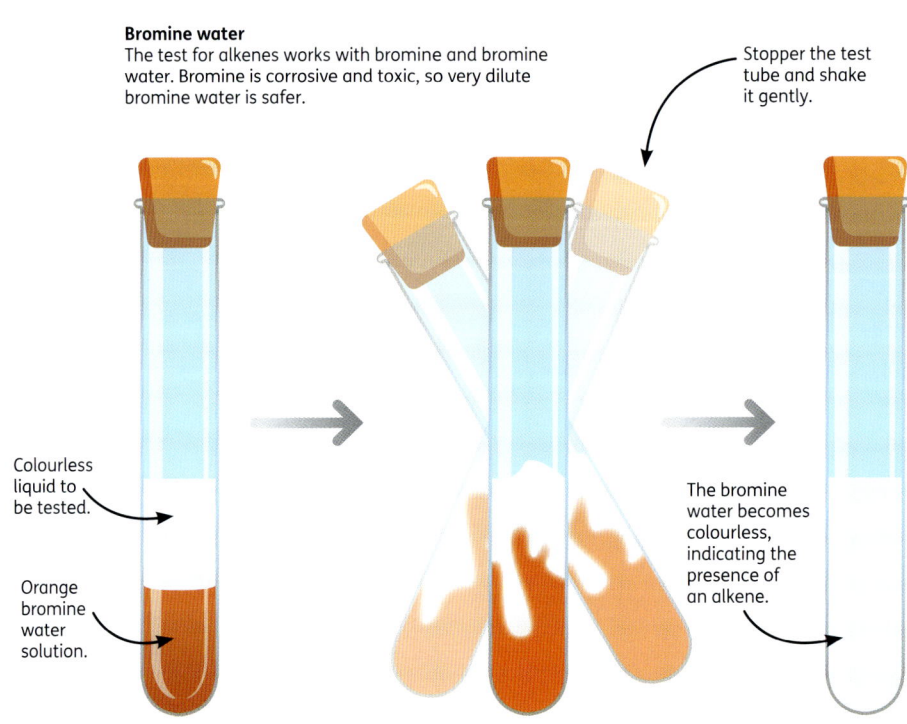

Bromine water
The test for alkenes works with bromine and bromine water. Bromine is corrosive and toxic, so very dilute bromine water is safer.

Colourless liquid to be tested.

Orange bromine water solution.

Stopper the test tube and shake it gently.

The bromine water becomes colourless, indicating the presence of an alkene.

Organic Chemistry

Alcohols

Key facts

- Alcohols are a homologous series of organic compounds.
- Alcohols possess the functional group –OH.
- Names of alcohols end with the suffix "-ol".
- The general formula for alcohols is $C_nH_{2n+1}OH$.
- Ethanol can be produced by fermenting sugars at moderate temperatures and pressures.
- Ethanol can be produced through the hydration of ethene (an alkene), which is an addition reaction that occurs at high temperatures and pressures.

Alcohols are a homologous series of organic compounds, which contain the functional group –OH. The first four alcohols are shown in the table below.

Properties of alcohols

Alcohols with short carbon chains are fully miscible with water, creating neutral solutions. Similar to hydrocarbons, alcohols undergo complete combustion in excess air or oxygen, resulting in the formation of carbon dioxide and water. Additionally, they can be oxidised to carboxylic acids through heating in the presence of oxidising agents.

Uses of alcohols

Methanol is toxic but can be used as a fuel, either on its own or with petrol. Ethanol is found in alcoholic drinks and is a useful biofuel. Ethanol can dissolve substances that water cannot. Ethanol kills bacteria so it is useful as an antiseptic.

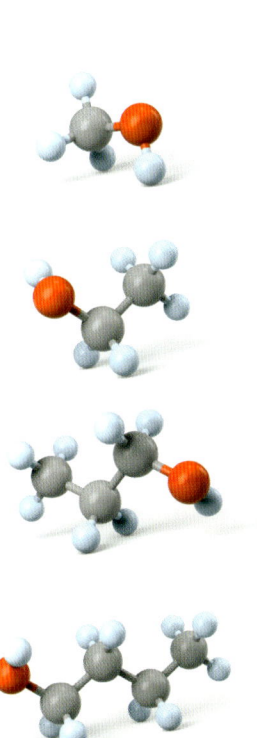

	Formula	Structural formula	Displayed formula
Methanol	CH_3OH	CH_3OH	H–C(H)(H)–O–H
Ethanol	C_2H_5OH	CH_3CH_2OH	H–C(H)(H)–C(H)(H)–O–H
Propanol	C_3H_7OH	$CH_3CH_2CH_2OH$	H–C(H)(H)–C(H)(H)–C(H)(H)–O–H
Butanol	C_4H_9OH	$CH_3(CH_2)_3OH$	H–C(H)(H)–C(H)(H)–C(H)(H)–C(H)(H)–O–H

Carboxylic Acids

Carboxylic acids are a series of organic compounds with the –COOH functional group, giving them similar reactivity.
Their formulae differ by a –CH2– group. The names of carboxylic acids end in "-anoic acid".

Key facts

- The carboxylic acids form a homologous series.
- Carboxylic acids all contain a –COOH functional group.
- Carboxylic acid names end in "-anoic acid" and have the general formula $C_nH_{2n+1}COOH$.

	Formula	Structural formula	Displayed formula
Methanoic acid	HCOOH	HCOOH	H–C(=O)–O–H
Ethanoic acid	CH_3COOH	CH_3COOH	H–C(H)(H)–C(=O)–O–H
Propanoic acid	C_2H_5COOH	CH_3CH_2COOH	H–C(H)(H)–C(H)(H)–C(=O)–O–H
Butanoic acid	C_3H_7COOH	$CH_3CH_2CH_2COOH$	H–C(H)(H)–C(H)(H)–C(H)(H)–C(=O)–O–H

Reactions of carboxylic acids

Carboxylic acids are weak acids, which react with reactive metals and carbonates, though more slowly than strong acids of the same concentration. The salts formed from these reactions end in "-anoate". The general equation for when a carboxylic acid reacts with a metal carbonate is shown here.

carboxylic acid + metal carbonate → metal salt + water + carbon dioxide

Esters

Esters are organic compounds formed by the reactions between alcohols (page 67) and carboxylic acids (page 68). They contain the –COO– functional group.
Esters have distinctive fruity aromas, making them useful in producing perfumes and flavourings.

Key facts

- Esters are organic compounds with a –COO– group.
- Esters are formed from alcohols and carboxylic acids.
- Sulfuric acid acts as a catalyst in their synthesis.

$$\text{alcohol + carboxylic acid} \xrightarrow{\text{sulfuric acid catalyst}} \text{ester + water}$$

Ethyl ethanoate

Ethyl ethanoate is an ester formed when ethanol is reacted with ethanoic acid. A small molecule of water is released for each ester molecule formed. Ethyl ethanoate is an effective solvent used in nail polish removers and adhesives.

Uses of esters

Esters are known for their fruity scents, making them popular in perfumes. They naturally occur in plants and are used in artificial flavourings.

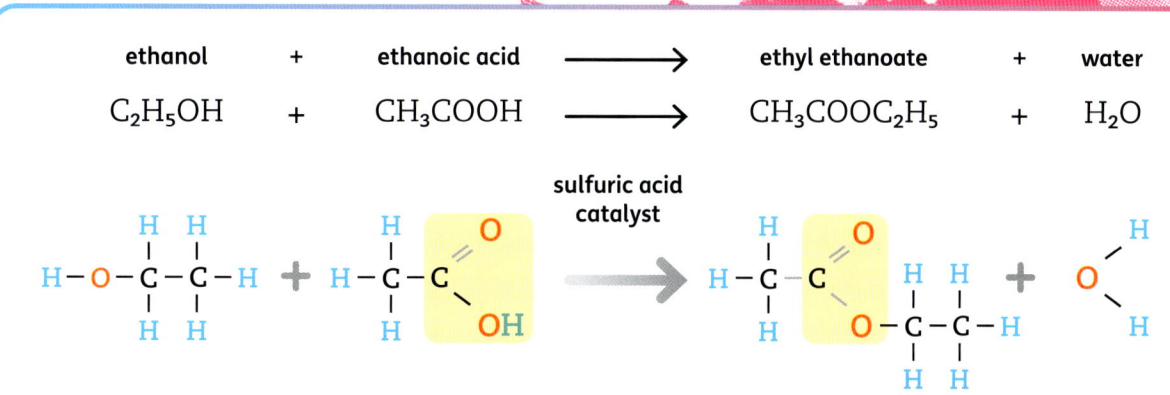

ethanol + ethanoic acid ⟶ ethyl ethanoate + water

$C_2H_5OH + CH_3COOH \longrightarrow CH_3COOC_2H_5 + H_2O$

Exam tip

When studying esters, remember that the name of an ester is derived from the alcohol and carboxylic acid it is formed from. For example, ethyl ethanoate comes from ethanol and ethanoic acid. This can help you write and recognise the chemical equations for esterification reactions more easily.

Organic Chemistry

Addition Polymers

Key facts

- Polymers are large molecules formed from monomers.
- Monomers must possess a carbon–carbon double bond.
- Addition polymerisation produces only the polymer.

Science skills

Whenever you are drawing the repeating unit for polymers, you must:

a) ensure the "n" is written on the bottom right of the repeating unit

b) make sure the two large brackets cross the bonds, which connect to other monomers.

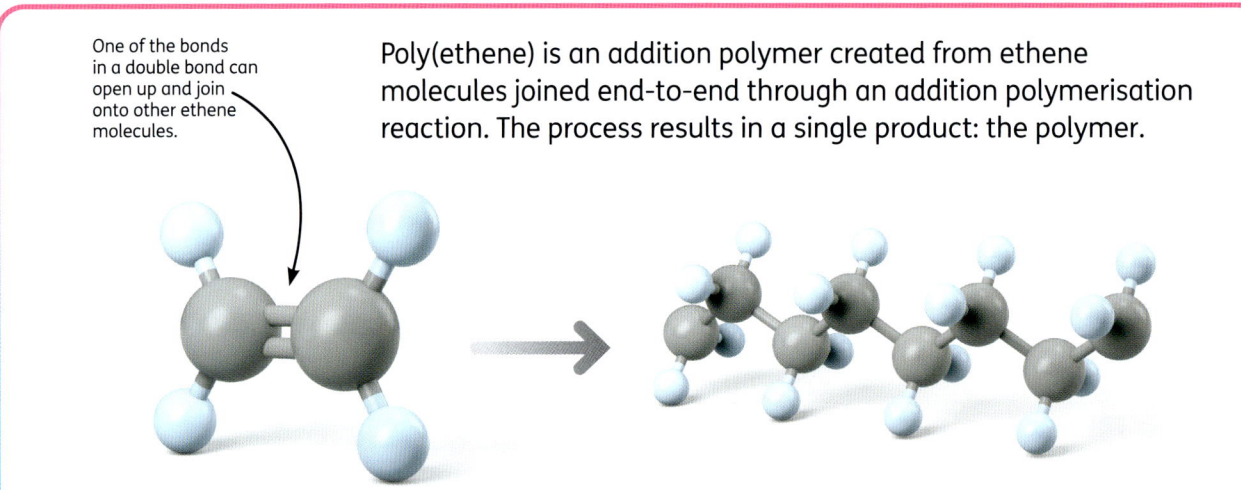

One of the bonds in a double bond can open up and join onto other ethene molecules.

Poly(ethene) is an addition polymer created from ethene molecules joined end-to-end through an addition polymerisation reaction. The process results in a single product: the polymer.

Addition polymerisation

Polymerisation reactions can be illustrated using displayed formulae, where each line represents a covalent bond. In the example shown, three ethene monomers join to form part of a poly(ethene) molecule.

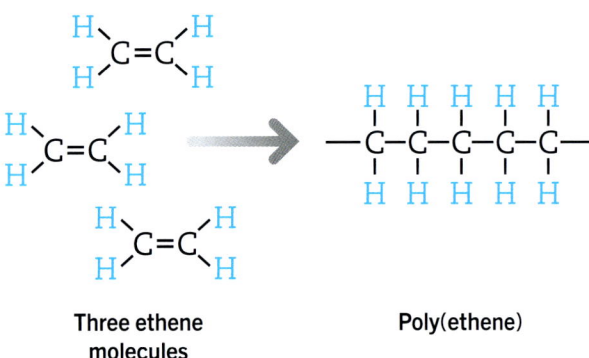

Three ethene molecules → Poly(ethene)

Repeating units

It would be impossible to draw some polymers fully, especially in the time constraints of an exam. Instead, we use a specific convention to represent a polymer. As a polymer molecule consists of repeating units, this is what we draw. Polymer molecules contain many of these units, so n is used instead of the actual number.

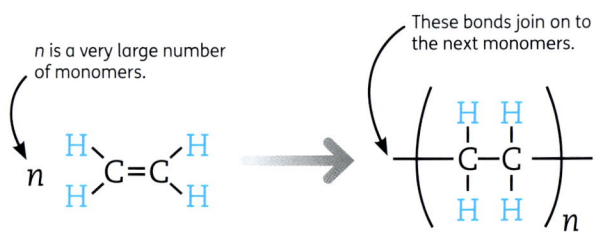

n is a very large number of monomers.

These bonds join on to the next monomers.

n ethene molecules → n repeating units of poly(ethene)

Organic Chemistry

Condensation Polymers

> **Key facts**
> - Condensation polymers consist of two distinct types of monomers.
> - These monomers do not require carbon–carbon double bonds (C=C) to form a polymer, but they must possess two functional groups.
> - The formation of each ester linkage in a polyester results in the production of one molecule of water.

Addition polymers, like poly(ethene), consist of one type of repeating monomer with C=C bonds, forming only the polymer. Condensation polymers, such as polyesters and polyamides, contain two types of repeating monomers, each having two functional groups. When these monomers combine, water is produced as a by-product.

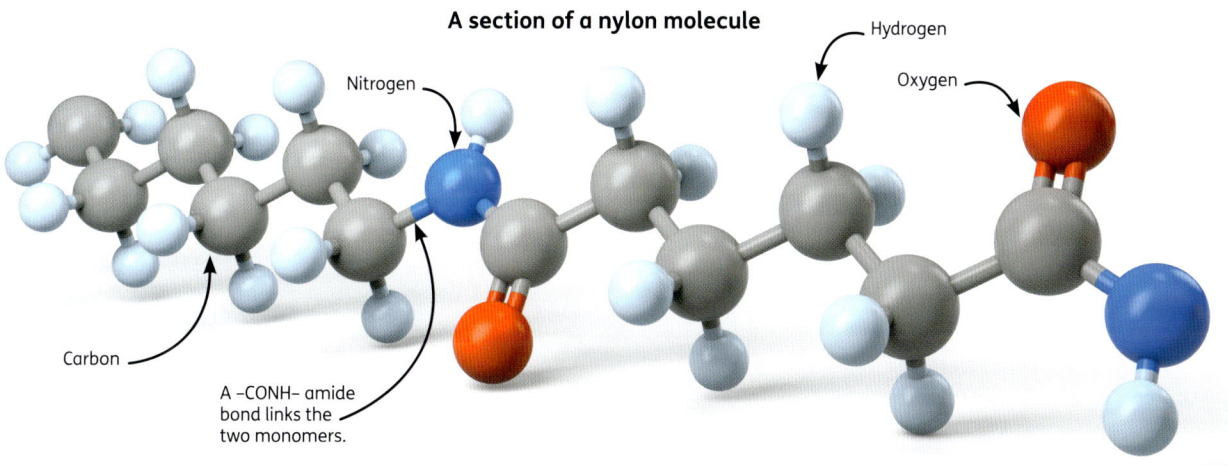

A section of a nylon molecule
- Nitrogen
- Hydrogen
- Oxygen
- Carbon
- A –CONH– amide bond links the two monomers.

Representing condensation polymers

Like addition polymers, there is a convention for representing condensation polymers. In a condensation reaction, two monomers join to form a polymer, producing a water molecule for each repeating unit. This diagram shows the condensation reaction between a carboxylic acid and an alcohol, forming an ester and water. Polyesters are formed when dicarboxylic acid molecules, which have one –COOH group at each end, react with diol molecules, which have –OH groups at each end. This reaction forms ester bonds (–COO) and releases water, creating the structure of the repeating unit shown here. The red and blue rectangles can represent any group of atoms; all that matters is that there are functional groups at both ends of the monomers.

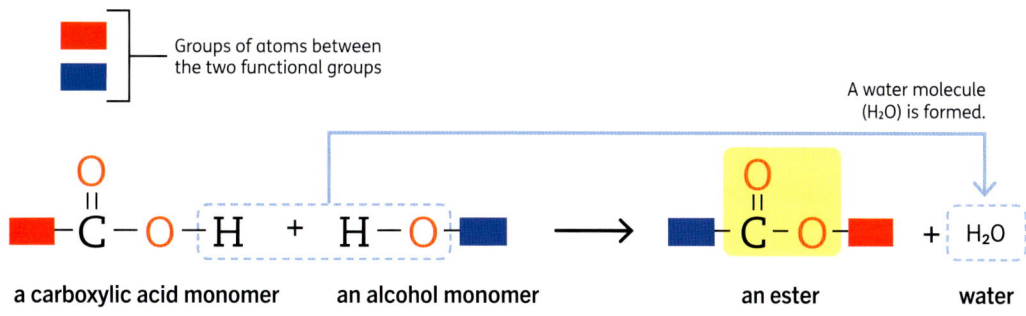

Organic Chemistry

Natural Polymers

Natural polymers are large molecules composed of repeated subunits found in nature. Examples include proteins, which are formed from amino acids, and DNA, consisting of nucleotide chains.

Key facts

- Proteins are condensation polymers made from amino acids; they contain peptide links.
- Different proteins consist of different combinations and numbers of amino acids.
- All enzymes are proteins.
- Starch and glucose are complex carbohydrates formed by multiple glucose molecules.

Proteins

Proteins are condensation polymers made from numerous amino acid monomers. Amino acids contain a –COOH functional group at one end and a –NH$_2$ functional group at the other end. These groups react to link the amino acids by forming peptide links. There are 20 standard amino acids. Examples of different types of protein include enzymes, hair and transport proteins.

Structure of proteins

Proteins are condensation polymers formed from amino acids. Amino acid molecules have distinct functional groups at each end, reacting to create peptide bonds, a type of amide bond (–CONH).

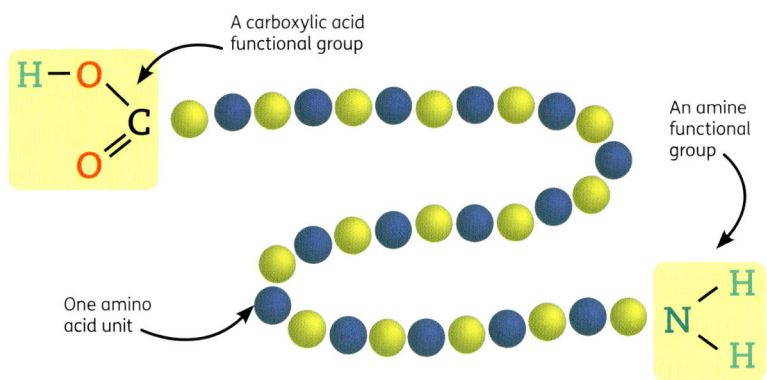

Other natural polymers

Natural polymers also include polysaccharides such as cellulose, starch and glycogen. These are all complex carbohydrates composed of repeated glucose units but differ in structure and function.

Cellulose	Starch	Glycogen
Cellulose is a structural polymer found in the cell walls of plants. Its rigid structure provides support to plant cells, making it a crucial component of wood, paper and cotton.	Starch is an energy storage polymer in plants. Starch is commonly found in staple foods such as potatoes, rice and corn.	Glycogen is a storage polymer in animals and fungi. In humans, glycogen is stored mainly in the liver and muscles, ready to be broken down into glucose when energy is needed.

Organic Chemistry

DNA

DNA is the genetic material located in the nucleus of a cell. It is composed of four different nucleotide monomers forming a condensation polymer. The DNA molecule consists of two strands that twist around each other to create a double helix structure.

Key facts

- DNA is composed of two strands forming a double helix.
- Each strand consists of nucleotides, which are made up of a sugar, a phosphate group and a base (G, C, A or T).

DNA double helix

The double helix structure of DNA resembles a twisted ladder, where the sugar and phosphate backbone forms the sides, and the paired bases (G–C and A–T) form the rungs. This configuration enables DNA to store genetic information efficiently and replicate accurately during cell division.

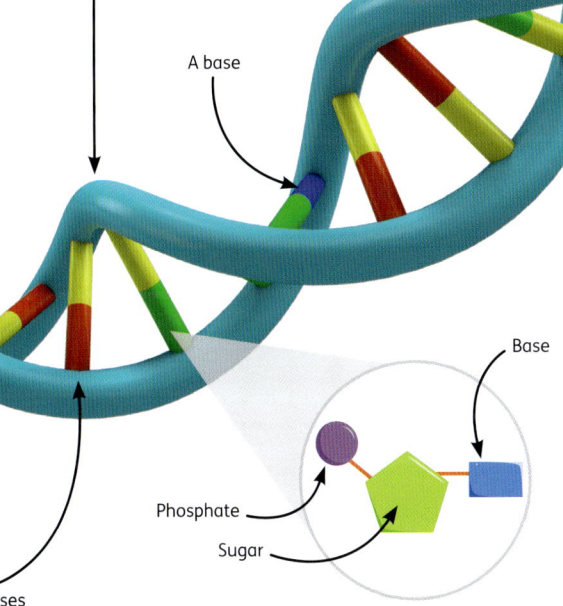

The structure of DNA

A nucleotide contains a sugar, a phosphate group and one of four bases: guanine (G), cytosine (C), adenine (A) and thymine (T). Hydrogen bonds link complementary bases from each DNA strand.

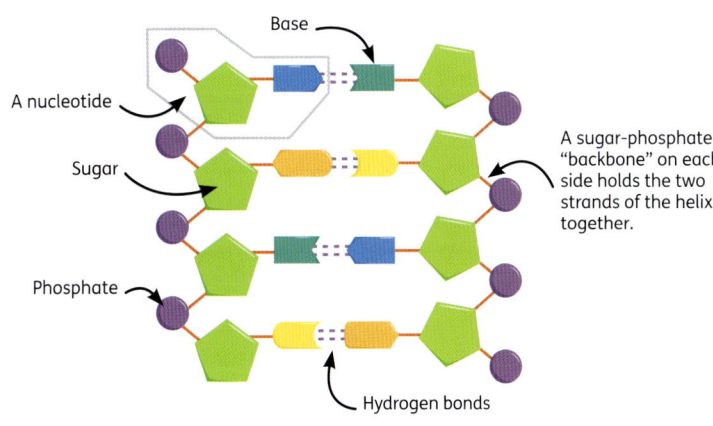

Brain Booster

Organic Chemistry Recap Quiz

 Find a pen and paper and work through these revision questions.

1. What is crude oil and how is it formed?
2. Define what an alkane is and give the name of the simplest one.
3. What are alkenes? Describe their general formula.
4. Explain the process of fractional distillation of crude oil.
5. What is cracking in chemistry?
6. Describe the structure and properties of alcohols and give an example.
7. Define carboxylic acids and give an example.
8. How are esters formed? Provide a reaction equation.
9. What is condensation polymerisation? How does it differ from addition polymerisation?
10. Explain the structure and function of DNA.
11. What are amino acids? Describe their general structure.
12. Explain the importance of esters in the food and fragrance industry.

Check your answers on page **110**.

Chemical Analysis

At the end of this chapter, you should be able to:

- ✓ Describe the characteristics of pure substances.
- ✓ Identify and describe common formulations.
- ✓ Describe tests to identify hydrogen, oxygen, chlorine and carbon dioxide gas.
- ✓ Describe how to carry out flame tests to identify the presence of specific metal ions.
- ✓ Explain the basics of spectroscopy and its application in chemical analysis.
- ✓ Describe how to detect the presence of metal ions using sodium hydroxide.
- ✓ Explain how to identify anions like carbonates, halides and sulfates.
- ✓ Recognise common errors in chemical testing and how to avoid them.

Chemical Analysis

Pure Substances

Key facts

- A pure substance consists of only one type of element or compound.
- Purity can be assessed by determining the melting or boiling point of a substance.
- Impurities typically lower the melting point and raise the boiling point.
- The closer the boiling and melting points of a substance are to those of its pure form, the higher its purity.

It is very common for people to think that only elements can be pure. Compounds can also be **pure substances** if they only contain one compound. For example, pure water consists of only water molecules. Most substances around us are not entirely pure. Tap water would not be described as pure as it contains dissolved ions with the water molecules.

How do we know if a substance is pure?

Purity can be checked by evaluating the melting and boiling points of a substance. Pure substances have specific melting and boiling points that do not change – these are known as **fixed points**. If the substance has impurities, its melting point will be **lower** and its boiling point will be **higher**. Comparing the observed melting and boiling points to those of the pure form can determine the level of purity.

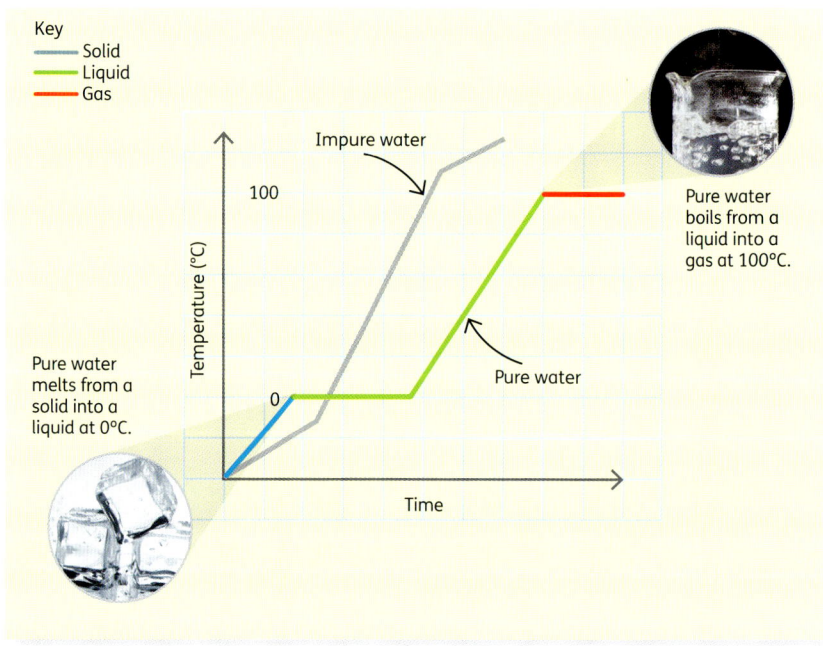

Pure water melts from a solid into a liquid at 0°C.

Pure water boils from a liquid into a gas at 100°C.

Salt and water

Salt and ice

Impure substances

Impure substances play a significant role in a range of everyday applications. For example, adding salt to water when cooking pasta helps to raise the boiling point, allowing the pasta to cook more evenly and quickly. Similarly, salt is spread on icy roads to lower the melting point of ice, making it easier for snow and ice to melt and thus keeping roads safer. Additionally, impurities in metal alloys, such as carbon in iron used to make steel, can enhance their physical properties for construction and manufacturing.

Chemical Analysis

Formulations

> ### Key facts
> - A formulation is a type of mixture that is created for a specific use.
> - Examples of formulations include medicines, baby milk, paint and laundry detergents.

A formulation is a mixture designed for a specific purpose, with each ingredient providing a unique property. Examples include nail polish, medicines, laundry liquid and paint.

Examples of formulations

Formulations are found everywhere in everyday life and are used in many different industries. Some common examples include:

- **Pharmaceuticals**
  Medications are formulated to ensure that they contain the correct dosage of active ingredients for therapeutic effectiveness. Other ingredients (excipients) are added to help with the delivery and absorption of the drug.

- **Cosmetics**
  Products like shower gels, lipsticks and shampoos are formulated to achieve desired textures, scents, colours and performance.

- **Cleaning products**
  Detergents and disinfectants are formulated to optimise their cleaning power and safely interact with various surfaces.

- **Foods**
  Some foods and drinks are formulated for taste, texture, nutritional content and shelf-life stability.

- **Paints**
  Specific formulations for paint can alter some of its properties, including durability, rapid drying and reduction of odour on application.

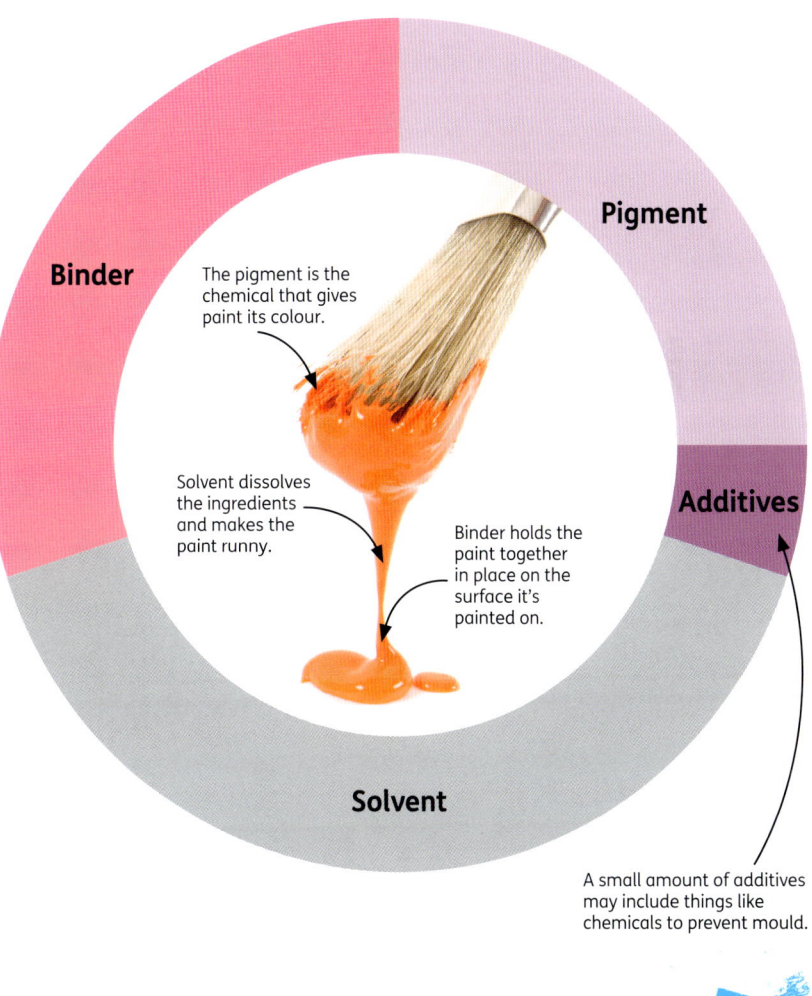

Chemical Analysis

Identification of Common Gases

> **Key facts**
> - Carbon dioxide turns limewater milky.
> - Hydrogen makes a squeaky "pop" with a lit splint.
> - Ammonia turns red litmus paper blue.
> - Oxygen relights a glowing splint.
> - Chlorine bleaches damp litmus paper.

Testing for gases is a fundamental aspect of chemical analysis. Each gas exhibits distinct behaviours when subjected to specific tests, providing reliable methods for detection.

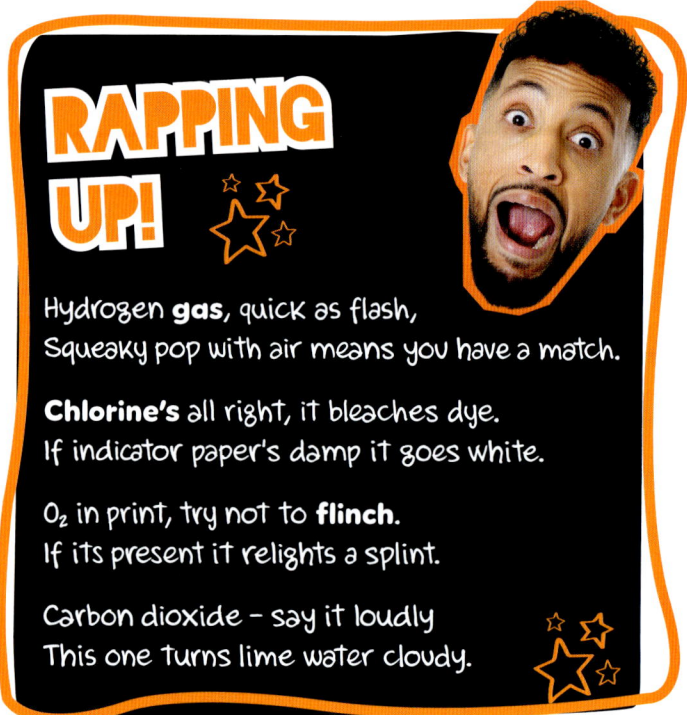

RAPPING UP!

Hydrogen **gas**, quick as flash,
Squeaky pop with air means you have a match.

Chlorine's all right, it bleaches dye.
If indicator paper's damp it goes white.

O_2 in print, try not to **flinch**.
If its present it relights a splint.

Carbon dioxide – say it loudly
This one turns lime water cloudy.

Testing for carbon dioxide gas

Carbon dioxide is naturally present in Earth's atmosphere, making up about 0.04 per cent of the air. It is required for photosynthesis and plays a significant role in the greenhouse effect, contributing to global warming.

Carbon dioxide is a non-toxic, colourless, odourless gas. It is relatively unreactive, slightly soluble and forms a weakly acidic solution. It can be detected in the laboratory using a splint, limewater or universal indicator.

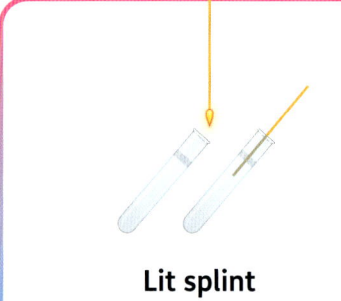

Lit splint
Insert a lit splint into one of the test tubes containing carbon dioxide gas. Observe that the gas will extinguish the flame.

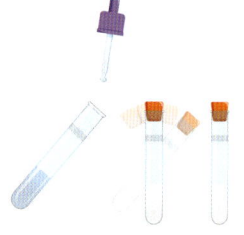

Limewater
Add limewater with a pipette to one test tube and shake. Carbon dioxide will turn the limewater milky.

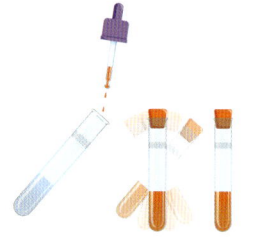

Universal indicator
Add a few drops of universal indicator to a test tube and mix thoroughly. Carbon dioxide, being mildly acidic, will cause the solution to turn red.

Testing for hydrogen gas

Hydrogen is a non-toxic, colourless, odourless gas. It is highly flammable and is used as a clean fuel source in various applications, such as fuel cells and rockets. Despite being the simplest element with only one proton and one electron, hydrogen plays a crucial role in the chemistry of life, particularly in the formation of water and organic compounds.

Hydrogen reacts explosively with oxygen. Using a lit splint in the presence of hydrogen gas will result in a squeaky pop sound being produced.

Chemical Analysis

Testing for ammonia gas

Ammonia is a compound of nitrogen and hydrogen and has the formula NH_3. It is a colourless gas with a pungent odour. Ammonia is commonly used in fertilisers, cleaning products and as a refrigerant. When ammonia is exposed to moist red litmus paper, it will turn the paper blue.

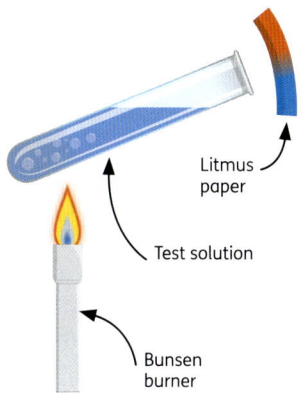

Testing for chlorine gas

Chlorine is a greenish-yellow gas with a strong, pungent odour. It is highly reactive and can be hazardous to health, causing respiratory issues and skin irritation. Chlorine is widely used as a disinfectant in water treatment and swimming pools due to its ability to kill bacteria and other pathogens. In a test for chlorine gas, moist blue litmus paper will turn red before eventually being bleached white.

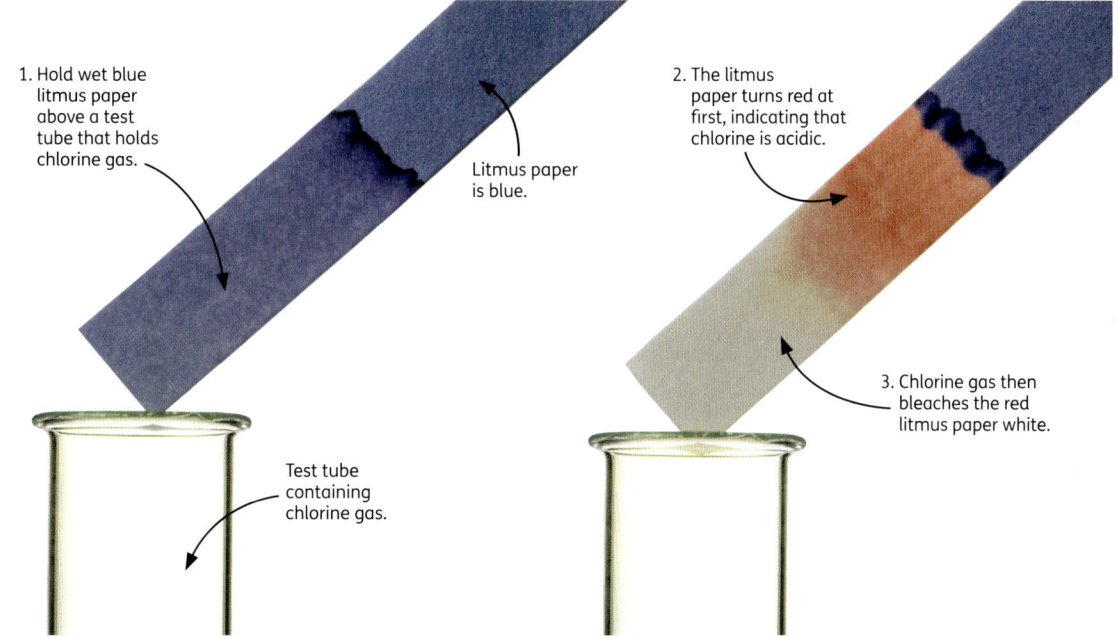

1. Hold wet blue litmus paper above a test tube that holds chlorine gas. Litmus paper is blue.
2. The litmus paper turns red at first, indicating that chlorine is acidic.
3. Chlorine gas then bleaches the red litmus paper white.

Test tube containing chlorine gas.

Testing for oxygen gas

Oxygen is essential for life and is the most abundant element in Earth's crust. It is a colourless, tasteless and odourless gas at room temperature. Oxygen supports combustion and is used extensively in industries such as steelmaking, as well as in medical applications and water treatment. The test for oxygen gas is to use a glowing splint, which will relight in the presence of O_2.

Exam tip

To remember the different gas tests effectively, try creating flashcards with the name of the gas on one side and the test for it on the other. For example, write "Ammonia" on one side and "Turns moist red litmus paper blue" on the other. Review these flashcards regularly and consider using mnemonic devices or associating each test with a vivid image to reinforce your memory.

Chemical Analysis

Identification of Cations and Anions

Key facts

- Cations are positive ions formed when atoms lose electrons.
- The presence of cations can be determined by a flame test or precipitate reactions with sodium hydroxide.
- The presence of cations can be determined by precipitate reactions.

Science skills

The flame test is testing for metal ions and not elemental metals. Metal ions are atoms that have lost or gained electrons, resulting in a net positive or negative charge. These charged particles can emit characteristic colours in a flame due to their unique electronic configurations. Elemental metals, on the other hand, do not undergo the same electron transitions, and their emission spectra can differ significantly from those of their ionic forms.

Flame tests

Flame tests can be carried out in a laboratory with a Bunsen burner and some nichrome wire. To carry out a flame test, follow these four steps:

1. Dip a clean wire loop into a sample of the metal compound you wish to test.
2. Heat the sample by holding the wire loop in the hottest part of a blue Bunsen burner flame.
3. Record the colour of the flame produced by the sample.
4. Compare the observed colour with known results to identify the metal ion present.

Ba^{2+} (Barium), Sr^{2+} (Strontium), Li^+ (Lithium), Na^+ (Sodium), Cu^{2+} (Copper), K^+ (Potassium)

Carbonates

When atoms gain one or more electrons in their outer shell, they form negative ions called anions. Carbonate ions (CO_3^{2-}) are commonly found in rocks such as limestone chalk. The test for carbonate ions is to add dilute hydrochloric acid. If carbonate ions are present, the hydrochloric acid will react with them to produce bubbles of carbon dioxide. Bubbling this gas through limewater will confirm the presence of carbon dioxide if the limewater turns milky.

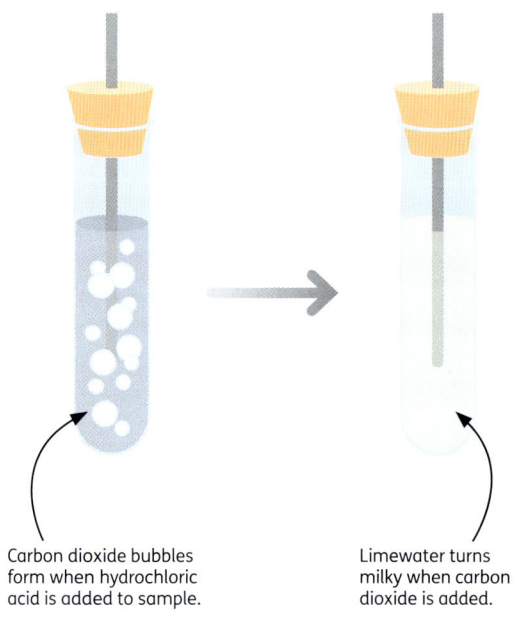

Carbon dioxide bubbles form when hydrochloric acid is added to sample.

Limewater turns milky when carbon dioxide is added.

Chemical Analysis

Precipitate reactions

Precipitates are small, insoluble particles that either float or sink in a solution. A precipitate forms when a dissolved substance in a solution reacts with another substance added to the solution, resulting in the production of an insoluble solid. If sodium hydroxide is added to a solution containing a metal, a metal hydroxide precipitate may form.

Al^{3+} Aluminium · Cu^{2+} Copper · Co^{2+} Cobalt · Fe^{3+} Iron(III) · Fe^{2+} Iron(II) · Zn^{2+} Zinc

Sulfates

Sulfate ions (SO_4^{2-}) are commonly found in many chemical compounds, such as salts (for example, sodium sulfate) and acids (for example, sulfuric acid). The test for sulfate ions is to add a few drops of dilute hydrochloric acid (HCl) or nitric acid (HNO_3) to the compound. This ensures that any other ions, such as carbonate ions, do not interfere by forming precipitates. Sulfuric acid cannot be used, otherwise you would be adding sulfate ions from the acid. A few drops of barium chloride or barium nitrate solution are added to the mixture. If sulfate ions are present, a white precipitate of barium sulfate ($BaSO_4$) will form.

Halides

Halide ions are negatively charged ions (anions) formed when halogen atoms gain an electron. You only need to know how to test for chloride, bromide and iodide ions. Halide ions are highly stable and commonly found in nature. For example, sodium chloride (NaCl), or table salt, contains chloride ions. The test for halide ions is to add a few drops of dilute nitric acid. This removes any interfering ions, such as carbonate ions, that might also form precipitates. A few drops of silver nitrate solution are added and the colour of any precipitate formed is observed.

Chloride ions produce white precipitate. · Bromide ions produce cream precipitate. · Iodide ions produce yellow precipitate.

Chemical Analysis

Instrumental Methods

Key facts

- Instrumental methods can detect and identify elements and compounds.
- Instrumental methods are characterised by their accuracy, sensitivity and speed.
- Flame emission spectroscopy is an example of an instrumental method used to analyse metal ions in solutions.

Exam tip

For exams, it's important to understand the principles of flame emission spectroscopy and other instrumental methods. This technique is valuable due to its high sensitivity and precision, offering advantages over traditional methods. Always check with your teacher or exam board which specific tests you need to focus on, as requirements can vary.

Modern instrumental methods offer several significant advantages over traditional flame tests and precipitate reactions. These methods, such as flame emission spectroscopy, provide enhanced accuracy, sensitivity and speed in detecting and identifying elements and compounds.

Flame emission spectroscopy

White light consists of red, orange, yellow, green, blue, indigo and violet. Metal ions in flame tests emit a mix of these colours. Flame emission spectroscopy separates these emitted colours to create a spectrum for each element. By analysing the emitted light, either visually or with a spectrometer, the type and concentration of metal ions in the sample can be determined. The diagram shows a simplified version of flame emission spectroscopy – the machine used in a laboratory would not look like this.

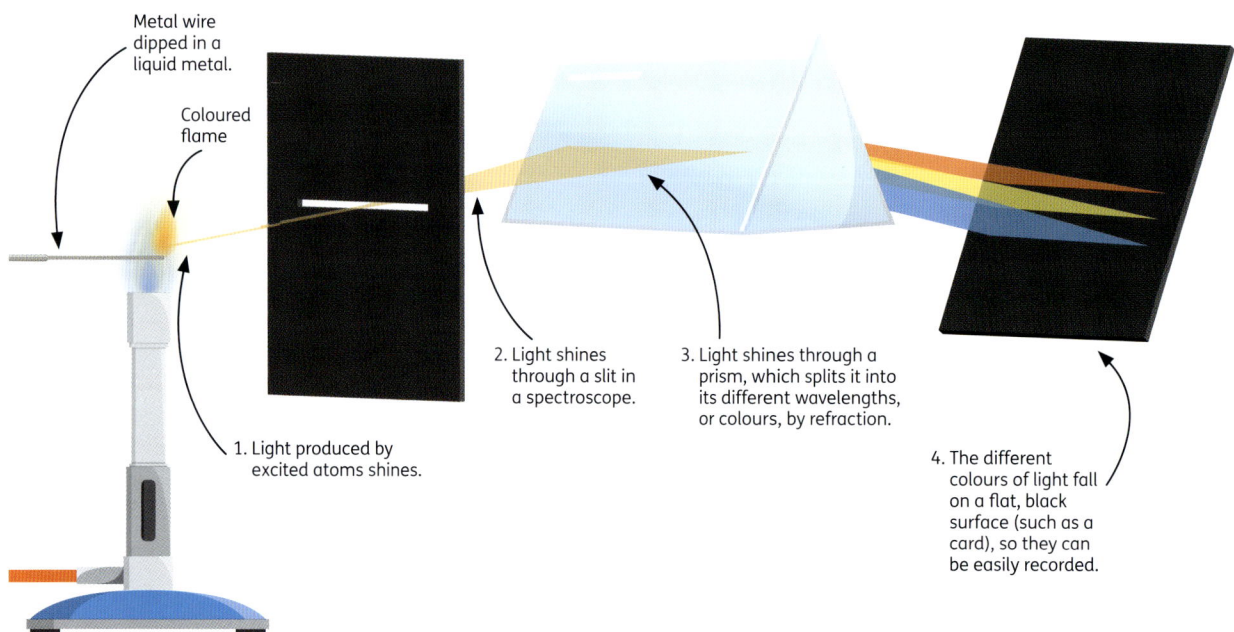

Chemical Analysis

Emission spectrum

When atoms are heated, their electrons gain energy and move to higher energy levels, emitting light of different colours as they return to their original levels. Each element produces a distinct spectrum, much like a fingerprint. These unique line spectra can be matched with a database to determine the metal ions present.

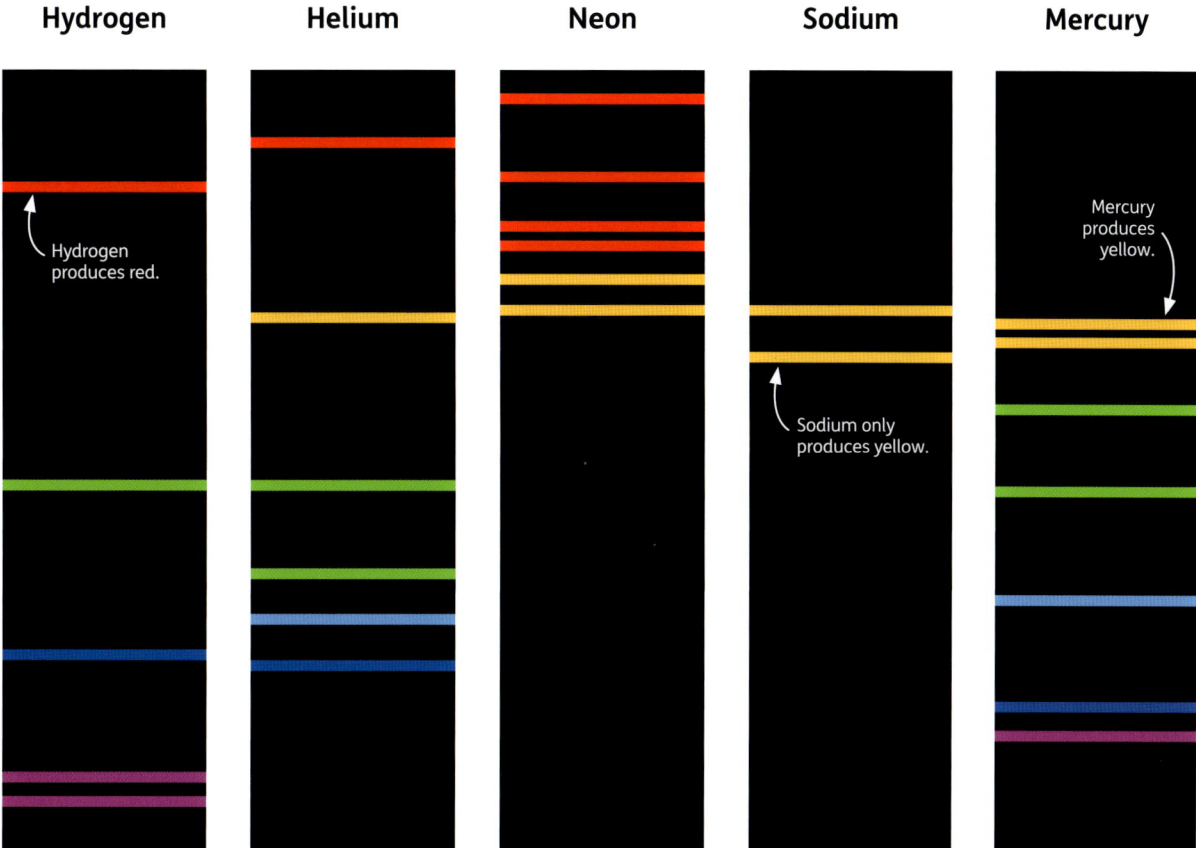

Advantages of instrumental analysis

Instrumental analysis offers several advantages over traditional chemical analysis methods.

Accuracy	Sensitivity	Speed
Instrumental methods are highly precise, allowing for the detection of elements and compounds at very low concentrations. This precision is crucial in applications where accurate measurements are essential, such as environmental monitoring and pharmaceuticals.	These methods can identify and measure trace amounts of substances that might be missed by flame tests and precipitate reactions. The high sensitivity ensures that even minute quantities of elements or compounds can be detected, which is important in fields like forensic science and toxicology.	Instrumental methods are faster than traditional techniques. They can quickly analyse multiple samples, which is valuable in industrial and research settings where time efficiency is critical.

Brain Booster

Chemical Analysis Recap Quiz

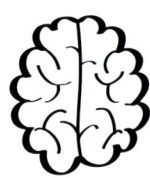

 Find a pen and paper and work through these revision questions.

1. What is the definition of purity in chemistry?
2. How can you determine if a substance is pure?
3. What is a formulation in chemistry?
4. Give **two** examples of everyday formulations.
5. Describe the test for oxygen gas.
6. How can you test for the presence of carbon dioxide?
7. What is the test for chlorine gas?
8. Explain how to test for ammonia gas.
9. Describe the test for hydrogen gas.
10. What is the flame test colour for sodium ions?
11. How can you identify aluminium ions using sodium hydroxide?
12. What colour precipitate indicates the presence of iron(II) ions when reacted with sodium hydroxide?
13. How can you test for carbonate ions?
14. Describe how to test for halide ions using silver nitrate.
15. List **two** advantages of instrumental analysis over traditional methods.
16. What is flame emission spectroscopy?

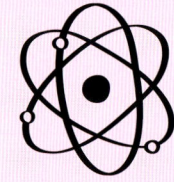

Check your answers on page **110**.

Chemistry of the Atmosphere

At the end of this chapter, you should be able to:

- ✓ Describe how the proportions of gases in the atmosphere have changed over time.
- ✓ Identify the primary greenhouse gases and their sources.
- ✓ Explain the greenhouse effect and its role in maintaining Earth's temperature.
- ✓ Explain the impact of human activities on the concentration of greenhouse gases.
- ✓ Describe the process and consequences of climate change.
- ✓ Describe the sources and effects of atmospheric pollutants from burning fossil fuels.
- ✓ Describe the role of renewable energy sources in reducing atmospheric pollutants.
- ✓ Explain the impact of deforestation on atmospheric composition.
- ✓ Explain what is meant by global dimming.

The Early Atmosphere

> **Key facts**
> - The atmosphere is composed of a mixture of gases that surround Earth.
> - Earth's early atmosphere predominantly consisted of carbon dioxide gas.

The composition of gases in our atmosphere has varied over time. There has been a marked change in the amounts in the atmosphere of two gases in particular: carbon dioxide and oxygen. It is these two gases that we need to focus on.

Earth's early atmosphere

When Earth formed 4.5 billion years ago, its surface was covered by **volcanoes**, which contributed to a very hot environment. The early atmosphere was created from gases released by volcanic eruptions and primarily consisted of **carbon dioxide**. Over billions of years, the levels of oxygen increased to reach their current state.

1. Volcanic eruptions
When Earth was newly formed, its surface was covered with numerous active volcanoes. These volcanoes released vast amounts of gases into the atmosphere, including carbon dioxide, ammonia, methane and water vapour.

Gas levels
carbon dioxide – large proportion of the atmosphere
oxygen – not present at all

2. Formation of oceans
As Earth gradually cooled, the intense heat from the volcanic activity began to reduce. The water vapour released into the atmosphere started to condense, forming clouds. These clouds eventually led to rainfall, which persisted over extended periods. The continuous rain accumulated and pooled in low-lying areas, leading to the formation of the first oceans.

Gas levels
carbon dioxide – still a large proportion of the atmosphere
oxygen – still not present at all

3. Life on Earth
Microorganisms, algae and plants first evolved in Earth's oceans, adapting to the aquatic environment. Over millions of years, they absorbed carbon dioxide from the atmosphere and released oxygen through the process of photosynthesis.

Gas levels
carbon dioxide – rapidly reducing in the atmosphere
oxygen – beginning to quickly increase in the atmosphere

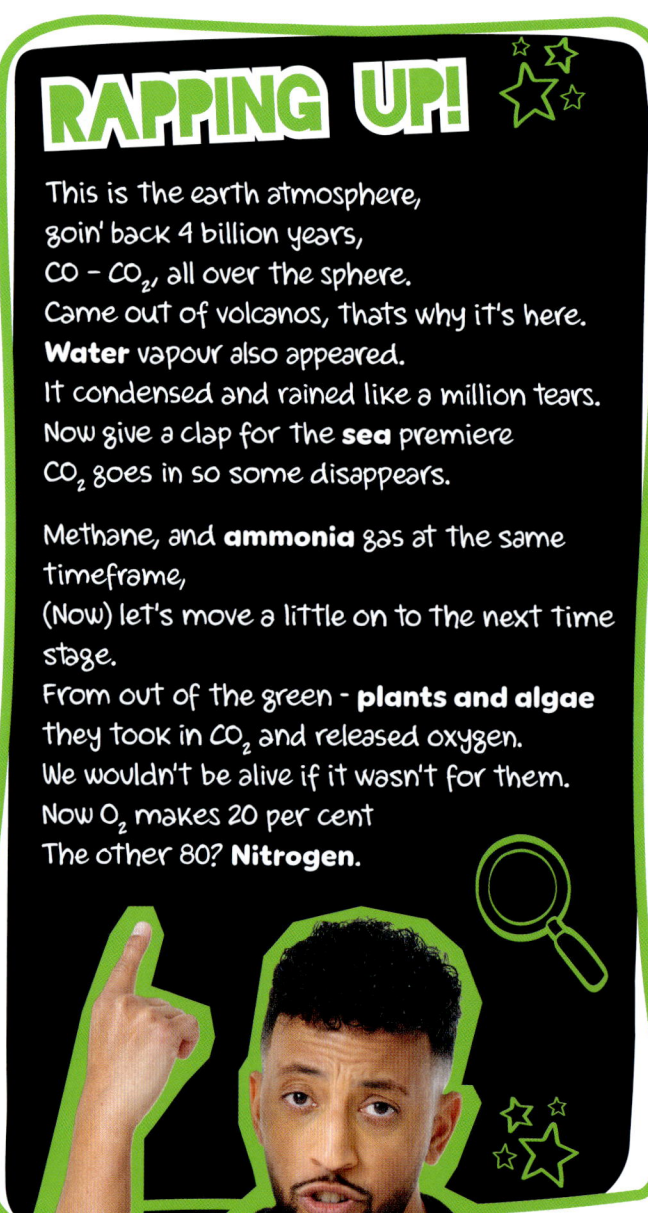

RAPPING UP!

This is the earth atmosphere,
goin' back 4 billion years,
CO – CO_2, all over the sphere.
Came out of volcanos, thats why it's here.
Water vapour also appeared.
It condensed and rained like a million tears.
Now give a clap for the **sea** premiere
CO_2 goes in so some disappears.

Methane, and **ammonia** gas at the same timeframe,
(Now) let's move a little on to the next time stage.
From out of the green – **plants and algae**
they took in CO_2 and released oxygen.
We wouldn't be alive if it wasn't for them.
Now O_2 makes 20 per cent
The other 80? **Nitrogen.**

Chemistry of the Atmosphere

The Current Atmosphere

Key facts

- The current atmosphere of Earth contains 78 per cent nitrogen, 21 per cent oxygen, less than 1 per cent argon, and tiny amounts of carbon dioxide and other gases.
- The current atmosphere is very different from Earth's early atmosphere.

Science skills

Students often misjudge the proportions of nitrogen, oxygen and carbon dioxide in our atmosphere. Remembering the exact values is helpful, but knowing the order from largest to smallest is essential. In exams, it's easy to mistakenly think oxygen or carbon dioxide are the most abundant gases due to their relevance to life and news.

The **composition of gases** in the atmosphere has developed over billions of years, creating the present-day mixture, which supports life.

The gases in our current atmosphere

The gases and their proportions in our atmosphere are shown in this diagram.

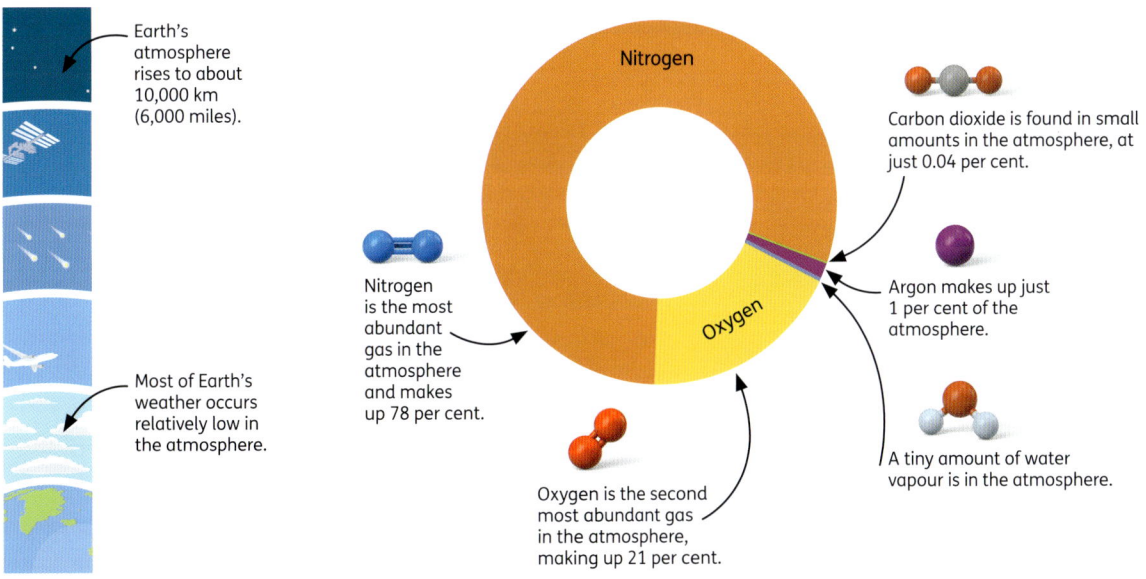

Nitrogen: 78 per cent
Nitrogen comprises 78 per cent of Earth's atmosphere due to its stability, which prevents it from being absorbed or transformed by geological or biological processes.

Oxygen: 21 per cent
Oxygen levels began to rise when algae started producing oxygen almost 3 billion years ago. Over time, plants evolved and the percentage of oxygen in the atmosphere increased, allowing animals to develop.

Carbon dioxide: 0.04 per cent
Carbon dioxide levels are at 0.04 per cent in the atmosphere due to its absorption by plants for photosynthesis, and the formation of carbonates in oceans and fossil fuels.

Chemistry of the Atmosphere

Global Climate Change

Key facts

- Greenhouse gases, such as carbon dioxide, methane and water vapour, trap heat from the Sun.
- Human activities increase greenhouse gas levels.
- Burning fossil fuels releases these gases, and deforestation reduces plants that absorb carbon dioxide.
- Human activity contributes to global warming by enhancing the greenhouse effect.
- Increasing the greenhouse effect is leading to an increase in global temperatures.
- Global warming drives climate change.

Human activity and greenhouse gases

Over the past three centuries, human activities have led to an increase in the levels of greenhouse gases in the atmosphere. Human activities that contribute to high levels of greenhouse gases include burning fossil fuels to generate energy for residential use and to operate vehicles, placing waste into landfill sites, deforestation and keeping an increasing number of farm animals. Human actions are also responsible for disrupting the natural carbon cycle, preventing the absorption of carbon dioxide from the atmosphere.

The greenhouse effect

The **greenhouse effect** warms Earth's surface naturally. When the Sun's energy reaches Earth, some is reflected back into space. The rest is absorbed and re-emitted by greenhouse gases like carbon dioxide, methane and water vapour. Without these gases, Earth's average temperature would be around −18°C, making survival difficult for most organisms.

The **greenhouse gases** (carbon dioxide, methane and water vapour) are small molecules connected by covalent bonds. Methane is especially potent because it traps more heat than other gases.

RAPPING UP!

Let me explain this quite direct –
we call this thing the **greenhouse effect**.

This effect all takes place quite near.
I'll list the steps now to make it clear.
Sun's **rays** enter the atmosphere,
it hits the earth's surface and warms up here.

Radiates it out as infrared.
Some leaves earth – some stays here instead.
What three things trap heat inside?
That's Methane, water and **carbon dioxide**.

This all leads to global warming.
The effect on earth is quite transforming.
Ice caps melt and sea level rise.
Rainfall changes and habitats die.

Last thing now is ya carbon **footprint**.
The big aim here is to make it shrink.
It's all the Carbon dioxide you put out
in life, and trust me it's more than you think.

Chemistry of the Atmosphere

Global warming refers to the gradual increase in Earth's average surface temperature due to human activities that enhance the greenhouse effect. This phenomenon is primarily caused by the emission of greenhouse gases, such as carbon dioxide and methane.

Effects of global warming

Many scientists believe that human activities could raise Earth's surface temperature, potentially resulting in global climate change. Modelling this complex system is challenging, often leading to simplified models. Global warming is associated with changes in climate patterns such as flooding, droughts and more severe storms.

How global warming happens

Greenhouse gases trap heat in the atmosphere, resulting in higher temperatures and climate changes. Human activities contribute to the increase of greenhouse gas levels in the atmosphere, which intensifies the greenhouse effect and raises global temperatures.

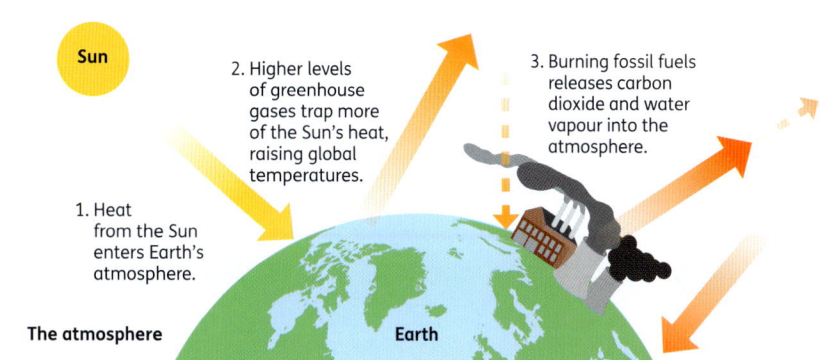

Flooding

Melting glaciers and ice caps contribute to rising sea levels, which can overwhelm coastal areas. Additionally, changes in land use and deforestation reduce the land's ability to absorb water, worsening flood conditions.

Drought

Climate changes can shift rainfall patterns, leading to less rain and extended dry periods. Higher global temperatures make arid regions hotter and drier.

Severe storms

Warmer temperatures result in more evaporation and moisture in the air, which leads to heavier rainfall.

Carbon footprint

A carbon footprint measures the greenhouse gas emissions produced by an individual, a product or a company. Factors like meat consumption and driving frequency can impact a person's carbon footprint. Diesel cars contribute significantly to carbon footprints due to their fuel combustion and exhaust emissions. Several factors contribute to an individual's carbon footprint. Gaining insight into your own carbon footprint can help you reduce it.

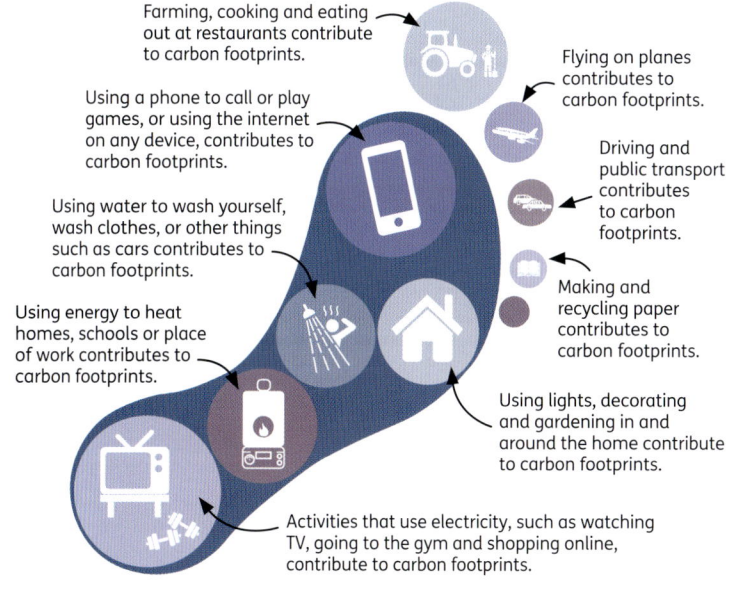

Chemistry of the Atmosphere

Air Pollution

Key facts

- Pollutant particles are toxic, causing breathing problems and potentially damaging buildings.
- Pollutant particles are usually colourless and odourless gases, making them hard to detect.
- Vehicles running on fossil fuels emit pollutants into the air.
- Fossil fuels contain hydrocarbons that create pollutants when burned, such as carbon monoxide, sulfur dioxide and nitrogen oxide.

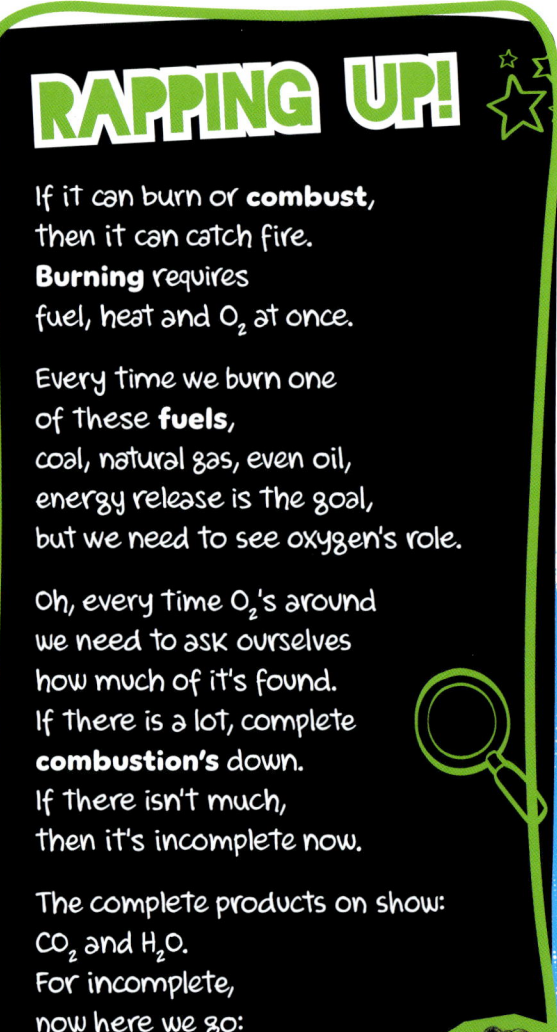

RAPPING UP!

If it can burn or **combust**,
then it can catch fire.
Burning requires
fuel, heat and O_2 at once.

Every time we burn one
of these **fuels**,
coal, natural gas, even oil,
energy release is the goal,
but we need to see oxygen's role.

Oh, every time O_2's around
we need to ask ourselves
how much of it's found.
If there is a lot, complete
combustion's down.
If there isn't much,
then it's incomplete now.

The complete products on show:
CO_2 and H_2O.
For incomplete,
now here we go:
swap this out for just CO.

The majority of vehicles around us continue to be powered by fossil fuels, including petrol and diesel. The combustion of these hydrocarbon fuels results in the emission of harmful pollutants and carbon dioxide, a greenhouse gas, into the atmosphere.

Complete and incomplete combustion

Complete combustion happens when a fuel burns with plenty of oxygen, producing carbon dioxide and water. **Incomplete combustion** occurs with insufficient oxygen, generating **carbon monoxide**, unburnt hydrocarbons and particulates. **Sulfur dioxide** (SO_2) and **nitrogen monoxide** (NO) form in vehicle engines through combustion. Burning fossil fuels like petrol or diesel causes sulfur to react with oxygen, creating sulfur dioxide. High engine temperatures cause nitrogen in air to react with oxygen, forming nitrogen monoxide. These pollutants contribute to air pollution and pose risks to health and the environment.

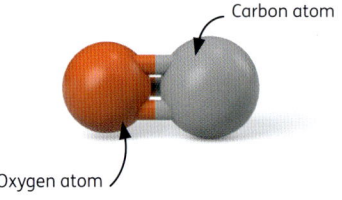

Carbon monoxide

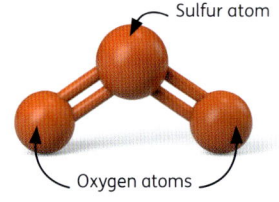

Sulfur dioxide

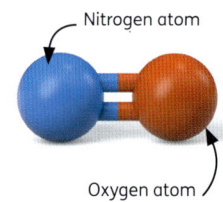

Nitrogen monoxide

Chemistry of the Atmosphere

Pollutant particles in the air can lead to long-term health issues. These particles are colourless, odourless and, generally, invisible. They can affect breathing and contaminate the blood. They may accumulate on buildings or obstruct machinery, and some are combustible, posing a fire hazard.

Acid rain

Rainwater naturally contains dissolved carbon dioxide, making it mildly acidic. However, pollution from gases like sulfur dioxide and nitrogen dioxide can significantly increase this acidity, leading to **acid rain**.

Although acid rain can occur naturally, such as in regions with **volcanic activity** or **decomposing vegetation**, both of which release carbon dioxide that acidifies rainwater, most acid rain is linked to human activities.

Acid rain can damage buildings.

Acid rain harms leaves, reducing the possibility of photosynthesis. This slows root growth, which, in turn, reduces the uptake of nutrients from the soil.

Acid rain can increase acidity of rivers or lakes, creating conditions in which most animals cannot survive.

Breathing problems

When humans inhale, haemoglobin in the blood binds to oxygen. Carbon monoxide molecules also bind to haemoglobin, inhibiting its capacity to transport sufficient oxygen, which can result in drowsiness, loss of consciousness or fatal outcomes. Carbon monoxide is odourless and colourless, making it difficult to detect.

Global dimming

Tiny pollutant particles in Earth's atmosphere block the Sun's light, causing global dimming. They scatter and absorb solar radiation, reducing the amount of light reaching the surface and decreasing photosynthesis by plants.

Exam tip

To remember the aspects of air pollution, use the acronym **PEAR**:

Particulates – refers to tiny particles causing global dimming

Emissions – include harmful gases like carbon dioxide and sulfur dioxide

Acid rain – results from sulfur dioxide and nitrogen oxides

Repercussion – denotes the environmental and health impacts of air pollutants

Brain Booster

Chemistry of the Atmosphere Recap Quiz

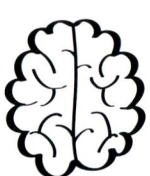

 Find a pen and paper and work through these revision questions.

1. What are the primary components of Earth's atmosphere?
2. What role did volcanic activity play in the early atmosphere?
3. Explain how oxygen increased in Earth's atmosphere.
4. State which processes contributed to the decrease of carbon dioxide in the atmosphere.
5. List the greenhouse gases.
6. How does the greenhouse effect impact global temperatures?
7. Explain some of the consequences of global climate change.
8. What is a carbon footprint and why is it important?
9. How does carbon monoxide form and what are its effects?
10. What is global dimming and what causes it?
11. How does acid rain form and what are its consequences?
12. How does nitrogen dioxide contribute to atmospheric pollution?

Check your answers on page **110**.

Earth's Resources

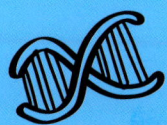

At the end of this chapter, you should be able to:

- ✓ Describe the methods used to produce potable water from fresh water sources.
- ✓ Explain the process of desalination and its importance in obtaining potable water.
- ✓ State the differences between potable water and pure water.
- ✓ Explain the importance of treating waste water before releasing it into the environment.
- ✓ Define life cycle assessment and its purpose.
- ✓ Identify the stages involved in conducting a life cycle assessment.
- ✓ Describe the process of corrosion and the factors that contribute to it.
- ✓ Explain the various methods used to prevent corrosion.
- ✓ Outline the steps involved in the Haber process for ammonia production.
- ✓ Explain the significance of the Haber process in agriculture and industry.
- ✓ Explain the role of NPK fertilisers in plant growth and agriculture.

Sustainable Development

Key facts

- Sustainable development involves the conservation of finite resources to ensure their availability for future generations.
- Finite resources are limited in supply and are subject to depletion.
- Fossil fuels, metal ores and minerals are categorised as finite resources.
- Renewable resources refer to substances that are inexhaustible.

Sustainable living conserves finite resources for future generations and utilises renewable energy sources. Many companies seek sustainability by minimising their use of limited materials through alternative methods.

Finite resources

Finite resources are those that are limited and can run out. Manufacturing depends on these resources, which include fossil fuels, metal ores and minerals. Fossil fuels like oil supply energy and raw materials for the chemical industry.

Renewable resources

Renewable resources can be quickly replenished from natural sources, making them excellent alternatives to finite resources. They include various types and can be reliably generated by natural processes without human intervention.

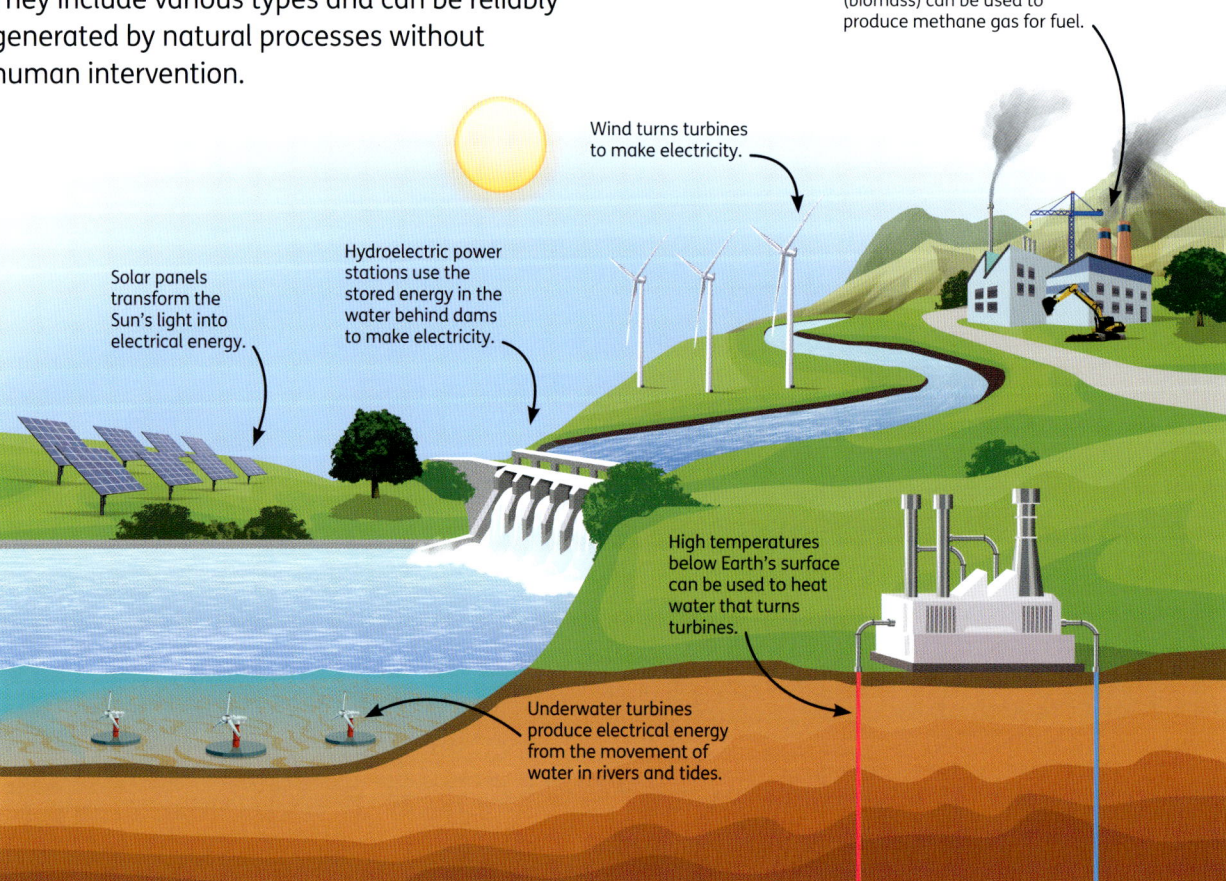

Fermenting plant material (biomass) can be used to produce methane gas for fuel.

Wind turns turbines to make electricity.

Solar panels transform the Sun's light into electrical energy.

Hydroelectric power stations use the stored energy in the water behind dams to make electricity.

High temperatures below Earth's surface can be used to heat water that turns turbines.

Underwater turbines produce electrical energy from the movement of water in rivers and tides.

Potable Water

Key facts

- Water from rivers, lakes and aquifers is stored in reservoirs.
- Natural water contains insoluble solids, soluble substances and bacteria.
- Potable water is safe for drinking.
- Seawater cannot be drunk due to its high salt content.
- Desalination turns seawater into pure water by evaporating and condensing the water vapour.

Potable water is suitable for drinking but is not pure. Potable water may still contain some dissolved substances. It comes from rivers, lakes and aquifers, which may have impurities like stones, leaves, mud, salts, fertilisers and microorganisms. This water is stored in reservoirs and treated for safe consumption as shown in the diagram.

Desalination

Approximately 97 per cent of Earth's water is contained within the oceans, rendering it unsuitable for consumption due to its high salt content (salinity). The process of desalination can convert seawater into potable water. Desalination is carried out in industrial facilities where seawater is passed through membranes to remove salt, or through simple distillation methods. Countries with hot climates and limited freshwater resources often establish desalination plants near coastal areas to produce drinkable water.

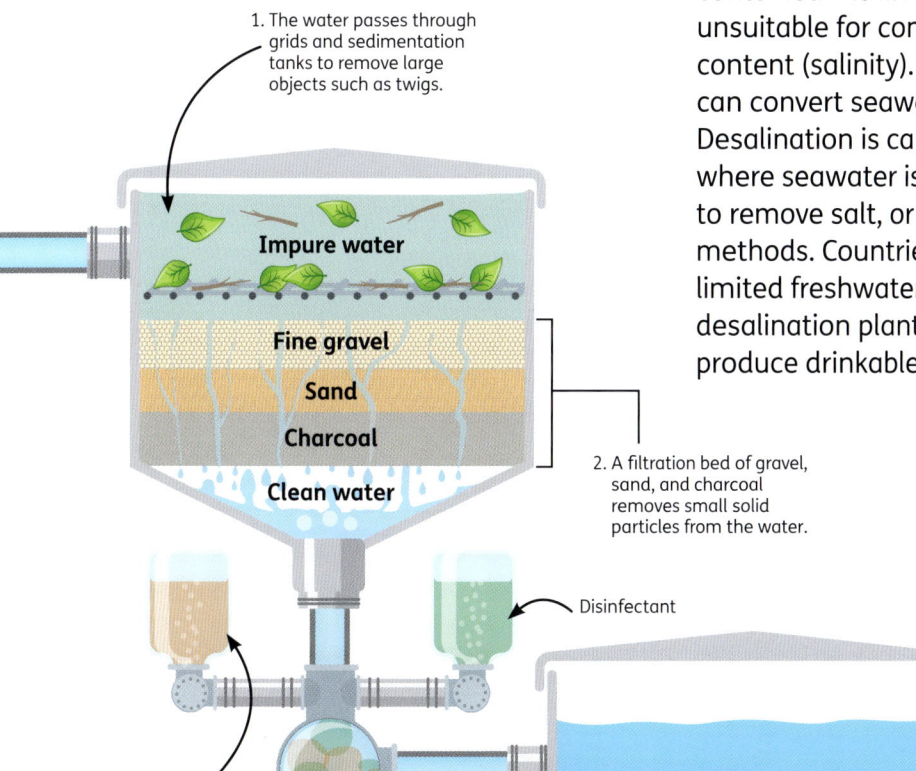

Treating Waste Water

Water is an essential resource used daily, yet a significant amount is wasted. Billions of litres are lost to drains and sewers. Waste water originating from industry, agriculture and residential areas contains harmful substances. For instance, residential waste water may contain bacteria that can cause diseases.

Key facts

- Waste water is purified at treatment centres by removing solids, chemicals and bacteria.
- Treated water can then be released into the environment.
- The main steps are screening, clarification, biological treatment, aeration and chemical treatment.

Residential waste water

This consists of water mixed with substances from toilets, drains and sinks. This includes organic matter like human and food waste, chemicals from cleaning products, soaps and detergents, as well as pathogens such as bacteria, viruses and parasites. Shower, bath and toilet water can contain nitrogen compounds like **ammonia (NH_3)**.

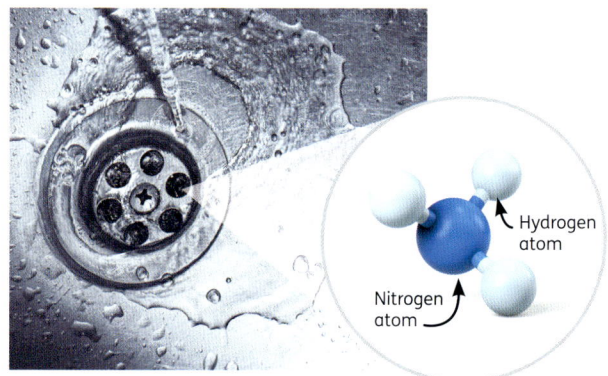

Ammonia molecule

Industrial waste water

This is produced by factories and often contains pollutants like **butane (C_4H_{10})**. These can damage the environment and poison wildlife if not treated properly. Treating industrial waste water is crucial to prevent contamination of nearby rivers and lakes, and harm to humans.

Butane molecule

Agricultural waste water

This is a by-product of farming activities, such as irrigation and pesticide application. It typically contains soil particles, organic matter, nutrients like **ammonium nitrate (NH_4NO_3)**, and various agricultural chemicals like pesticides and herbicides. It can contaminate nearby water bodies, leading to **eutrophication** which affects aquatic life.

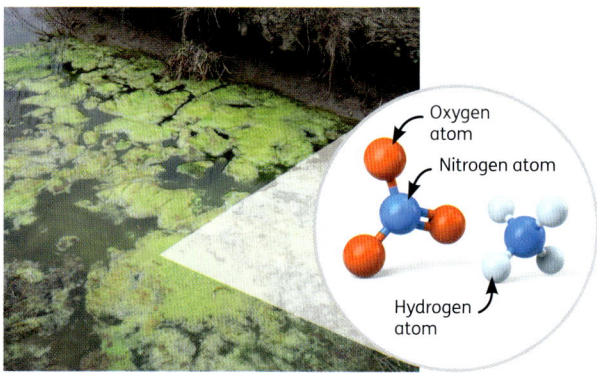

Ammonium nitrate (NH_4NO_3), molecules

Earth's Resources

Treating waste water

Treating waste water is essential to remove harmful substances and microorganisms that can pose health risks to humans and aquatic life. If untreated, pollutants from residential, industrial and agricultural sources can contaminate water bodies, leading to environmental damage and the poisoning of wildlife. Proper treatment processes ensure that the water is safe for **discharge** into the environment, preventing the spread of diseases, and maintaining ecological balance.

Sewage treatment

Sewage treatment removes harmful substances and microorganisms from waste water. The primary stage separates large solids through **screening** and **sedimentation**. Biological treatments then break down organic matter with **bacteria**. Next, advanced filtration and **chemical treatments** remove any remaining impurities and pathogens. Finally, effluent is discharged safely into the environment. The **sludge** can be used as fertiliser or burnt to generate electricity.

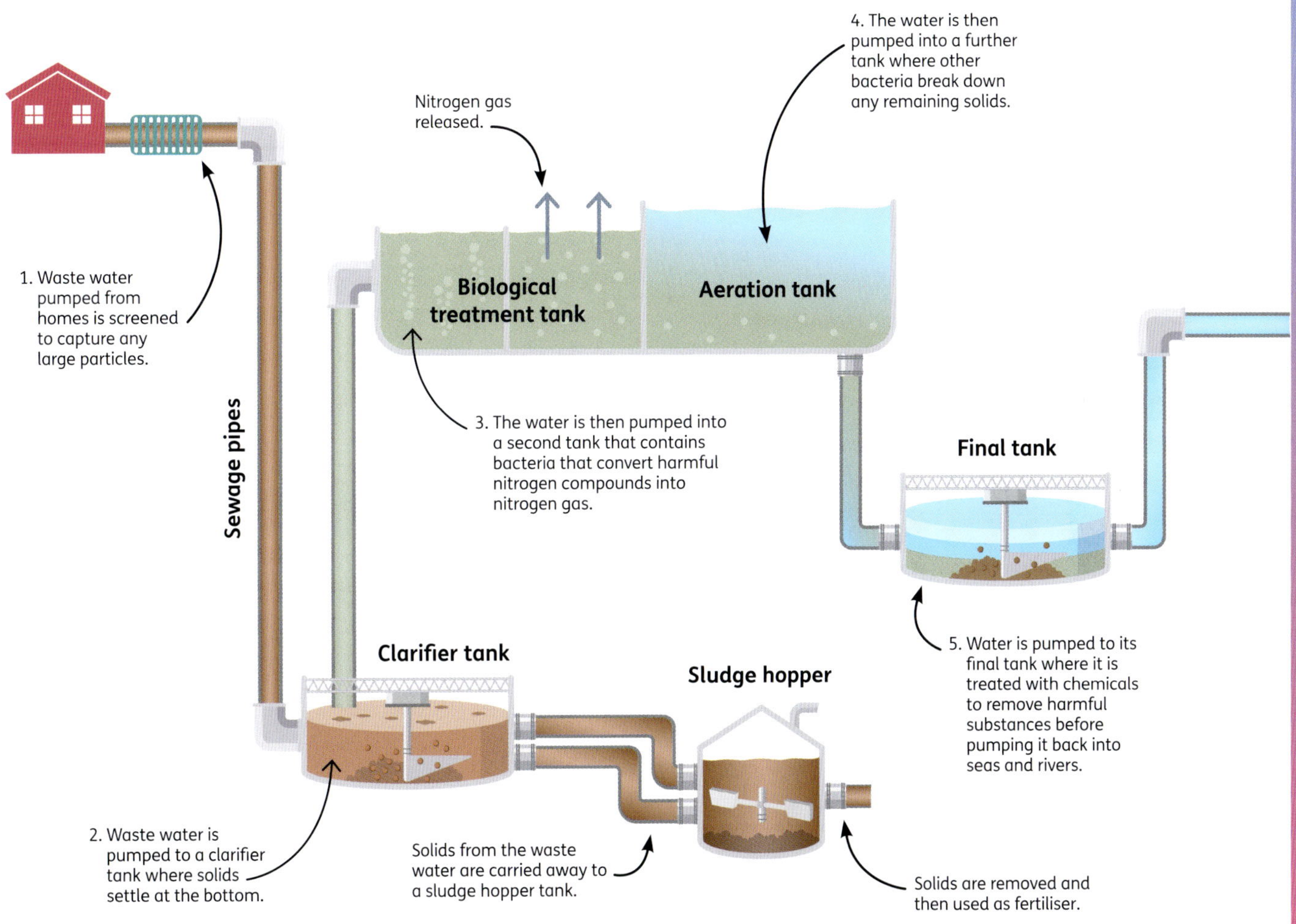

1. Waste water pumped from homes is screened to capture any large particles.

2. Waste water is pumped to a clarifier tank where solids settle at the bottom.

3. The water is then pumped into a second tank that contains bacteria that convert harmful nitrogen compounds into nitrogen gas.

4. The water is then pumped into a further tank where other bacteria break down any remaining solids.

5. Water is pumped to its final tank where it is treated with chemicals to remove harmful substances before pumping it back into seas and rivers.

Nitrogen gas released.

Biological treatment tank

Aeration tank

Sewage pipes

Clarifier tank

Sludge hopper

Final tank

Solids from the waste water are carried away to a sludge hopper tank.

Solids are removed and then used as fertiliser.

Exam tip

You could be asked to recall any of the waste water treatment techniques in your exam. Search online for videos using the search phrase "Treating Waste Water"; add "GCSE" into your search to narrow down the results to material that is targeted at your exam. Pause the video in appropriate places and make a flashcard of each stage.

Alternative Metal Extraction

Key facts

- Copper ores are increasingly rare, prompting scientists to develop methods for extracting copper from low-grade ores.
- Bioleaching and phytomining are two approaches used to obtain copper in an environmentally responsible manner.

Processing metals

Metal can be extracted from compounds, such as obtaining copper from copper solutions through displacement with scrap iron or electrolysis.

Bioleaching

Bacteria can extract copper from low-grade ores. This is cheaper and less harmful to the environment than mining high-grade ores. The process, called bioleaching, uses bacteria to produce leachate solutions (acidic liquids) containing metal compounds, making it a more sustainable alternative.

Phytomining

Plants grown in copper-rich soils absorb the copper into their roots, which is then transported to their leaves. The copper can be extracted by burning the leaves and collecting the ash, which contains soluble copper compounds. This method is called phytomining, and is both economical and sustainable as it uses little energy and none of the natural reserves of copper ores.

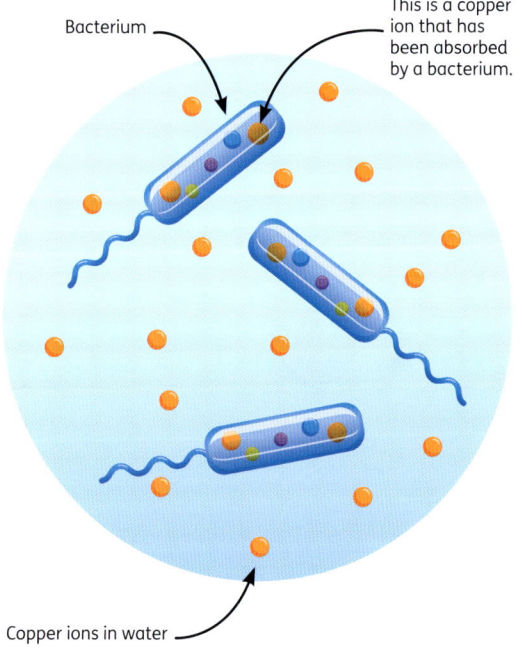

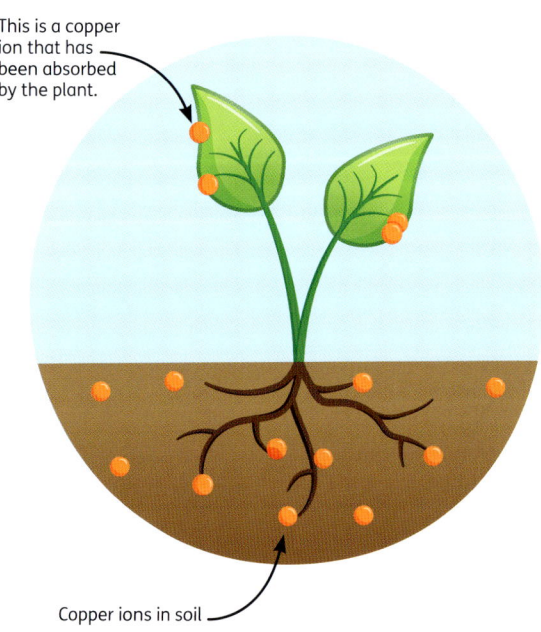

Exam tip

Remember that bioleaching uses bacteria, whilst phytomining involves growing plants.

Ceramics

Ceramics, including china, bricks and glass, are non-metallic materials held together by covalent or ionic bonds or a combination of both. Ceramics are produced by heating components to high temperatures. They share properties such as high melting points, stiffness, brittleness, strength and good insulation.

Key facts

- Ceramics are non-metal materials created by heating substances at high temperatures.
- They can have covalent or ionic bonds, including metals bonded to non-metals.
- Ceramics are known for their high melting points, heat resistance, inertness, stiffness, brittleness, strength and insulating properties.

Types of ceramics

Ceramics can be divided into three groups.

Pottery
Various types of clay are moulded into specific shapes or objects, then are subjected to temperatures reaching 1,000°C (1,832°F).

During the heating and cooling processes, chemical reactions take place, and these facilitate the bonding of molecules within the ceramic material. The final stages are traditionally glazing and decorating.

Bricks
Clay containing various impurities is shaped, dried and subsequently subjected to a temperature of 1,200°C (2,192°F).
The presence of different impurities results in bricks of varying colours.

Glass
There are two main types of glass:

- Soda-lime glass is created by heating a mixture of silicon dioxide, sodium carbonate and calcium carbonate to 1,600°C (2,912°F). This type of glass is widely used due to its cost-effectiveness.

- Borosilicate glass is made by heating silicon dioxide and boron oxide. It is useful for experiments due to its ability to resist rapid temperature changes.

Reduce, Reuse, Recycle

Key facts

- Reduce, reuse and recycle are three fundamental principles in environmental conservation aimed at minimising waste and conserving resources.
- Recycling means using materials more than once.
- Reduce means to reduce waste by using resources more efficiently.
- Reuse means to repurpose items rather than discarding them after one use.

Essential principles for reducing waste and conserving resources are **reduce**, **reuse** and **recycle**, ensuring a sustainable future.

Reduce
This concept involves reducing waste by selecting products with minimal packaging, purchasing in bulk and avoiding disposable items. It promotes efficient use of resources and mindful consumption.

Reuse
Reuse involves repurposing items for the same or different uses, such as using a jar for storage, or donating clothes. This extends product life and reduces the need for new resources.

Recycle
Recycling involves processing used materials into new products to prevent waste and reduce the use of raw materials. Through recycling, materials such as paper, glass, plastic and metals can be transformed and reused, reducing the strain on finite resources and saving energy and fossil fuels.

Recycling glass

Glass recycling is straightforward, saving both time and money while producing a product nearly identical to new glass.

1. Glass is collected at recycling points.
2. The glass is sorted by colour and type, and crushed.
3. The crushed glass is mixed together and heated until it melts.
4. The glass is formed into sheets.
5. The glass sheets are then shaped into bottles.
6. The recycled glass bottles are ready to be used again.

Recycling metals

Metals are recycled by melting and reshaping them, similar to glass. Chemical treatments may be used to remove impurities.

Life Cycle Assessment

To evaluate the environmental impact of a product throughout its life cycle, a **life cycle assessment (LCA)** is used. LCAs can be time-consuming but provide valuable insights into the efficiency and sustainability of products. They help people to make informed decisions about the products they use, and encourage the exploration of more sustainable options.

> **Key facts**
>
> - A life cycle assessment (LCA) evaluates the environmental impact of a product.
> - An LCA encompasses five areas: extraction of raw material, manufacturing, usage, disposal, and transport between each area.

Life cycle assessment stages

An LCA considers five main areas:

1. The extraction of raw materials
2. Manufacturing and processing
3. Our usage of the product
4. Disposal
5. Transport

Comparing LCAs

When evaluating the LCA of plastic bags compared to paper bags, it may appear that plastic bags have a greater environmental impact. There are well-documented challenges associated with their disposal, because they are non-biodegradable. However, a lot of energy is used during the production of paper bags, and it also generates considerable waste. It can potentially contribute to deforestation.

Problems with LCAs

Certain types of energy and resource usage are straightforward to quantify. Other effects are more challenging. This introduces subjective judgements in LCAs, which may lead to biases.

Corrosion

When exposed to air, metals form a dull coating due to corrosion from reactions with gases like oxygen. Sodium corrodes quickly, forming sodium oxide, while silver corrodes slowly, creating silver oxide.

Rusting

Rusting is a specific type of corrosion that affects iron and its alloys. It occurs when iron reacts with oxygen and moisture in the environment, leading to the formation of iron oxide, commonly known as rust. This reddish-brown compound progressively weakens the metal.

Rust appears on iron nails as a rough, red layer.

Key facts

- Corrosion refers to the chemical reaction between a metal surface and its surrounding environment.
- Metals that have higher reactivity tend to corrode at an accelerated rate.
- When a metal undergoes corrosion in the presence of air, it often results in the formation of a layer of metal oxide.
- Rusting is a particular form of corrosion that affects iron.

Aluminium corrosion

Aluminium reacts with oxygen in the air to form a layer of aluminium oxide. This type of corrosion differs from rust, as it does not crumble or erode. The layer adheres to aluminium and prevents further corrosion.

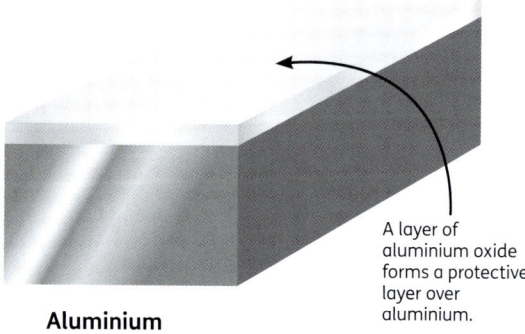

Aluminium

A layer of aluminium oxide forms a protective layer over aluminium.

Science skills

You need to recall the word equation for rusting:

iron + oxygen + water → hydrated iron(III) oxide

Hydrated iron(III) oxide is what we call rust. You can see how rust can only refer to iron: the compound formed is an oxide of iron.

Preventing Corrosion

Corrosion often leads to metals needing to be replaced at significant cost. Protective coatings shield the metal from air and moisture. The coating used depends on the specific object. For example, machinery and tools are usually coated with oil or grease, while vehicles are protected with paint.

Key facts

- Corrosion leads to the deterioration of metals.
- Various types of coating prevent corrosion by providing a barrier against air and water, including oil, grease, paint, tin plating and electroplating.

Preventing iron from rusting

Various environments influence the formation of rust on an iron nail. To prevent rusting, either water or oxygen must be removed from contact with the iron.

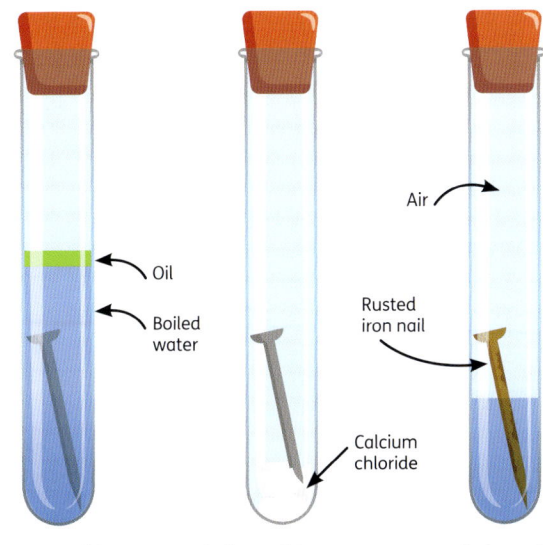

An iron nail in a test tube of boiled water under oil won't rust – the layer of oil stops air reaching it.

An iron nail in a test tube with calcium chloride will not rust, because calcium chloride absorbs water vapour from the air.

An iron nail will rust if placed in a test tube containing both water and air.

Water present: no oxygen	No water: oxygen present	Water present: oxygen present
An iron nail in boiled water under oil does not rust because the oil layer prevents air from reaching it. Boiling the water removes any oxygen present.	An iron nail in a test tube with calcium chloride will not rust as calcium chloride absorbs water vapour from the air.	An iron nail will rust when it is exposed to water and air. The mass of the nail increases because the iron atoms bond with the oxygen and water molecules, producing a new substance – iron(III) oxide.

Protecting metal

Several methods prevent the corrosion of metals:

- **Coating:** applying a protective layer can prevent exposure to air and moisture.
- **Galvanisation:** covering iron or steel with a layer of zinc helps to prevent rust as the zinc corrodes instead of the iron.
- **Electroplating:** using electrical current to coat metal surfaces with another metal.
- **Use of alloys:** combining metals to create alloys like stainless steel, which is less susceptible to rusting.

Alloys

> **Key facts**
> - Alloys are mixtures of metals with other elements.
> - Alloys typically possess more useful properties than the pure metals.
> - Alloys can be stronger, harder, lighter or less prone to corrosion.

An **alloy** is a mixture of a metal with small quantities of other metals or non-metals. Alloys may have different properties compared to the pure metals they consist of, making them applicable in various contexts. **Bronze**, which is an alloy of copper and tin, exhibits increased strength compared to either of the pure metals alone.

Aluminium alloys

Bicycle frames are constructed using an **aluminium alloy** that contains magnesium and silicon, providing both lightness and strength.

Copper alloys

Trumpets are constructed from copper-zinc alloys known as **brass**, which are durable and resistant to corrosion.

Gold alloys

Watches and jewellery made with titanium-gold alloys are stronger and harder than those made from pure gold. Gold used in jewellery is typically an alloy that includes silver, copper and zinc. The proportion of gold in the alloy is measured in carats, with 24 carat indicating 100 per cent pure gold, and 18 carat indicating 75 per cent gold.

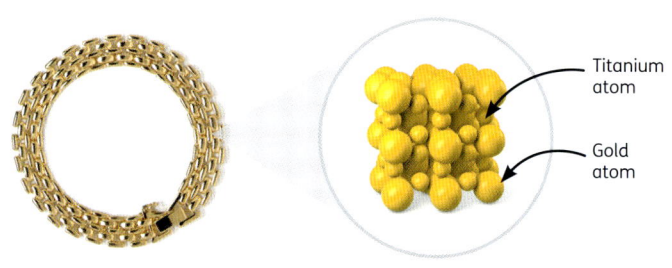

Steel

Cutlery is made of **stainless steel**, an alloy of iron and chromium that resists corrosion. Steels are alloys of iron that contain specific amounts of carbon and other metals. **High carbon steel** has high strength but is brittle. **Low carbon steel** is softer and easier to shape.

Composites and Polymers

Key facts

- Composites are made from one substance embedded in another's fibres.
- Composite properties depend on the materials used.
- Plastic polymers come in two types: thermosoftening and thermosetting.

Composites are materials made by embedding one substance in another's fibres. They combine the properties of each component, making them suitable for specific applications.

Fibreglass and carbon fibre

Glass or carbon fibres embedded in polyester resin create strong composites. Fibreglass is easily shaped, strong, light, and slightly flexible. Carbon fibre is stronger and lighter but more expensive.

Concrete

Concrete, composed of sand, cement and aggregate, is a strong material used in buildings. Reinforced concrete has steel rods embedded in it for added strength.

Natural composite

Cellulose fibres embedded in a natural polymer called lignin in wood is an example of a natural composite. This combination is much stronger than the separate substances on their own.

Types of polymer

The characteristics of polymers are influenced by the types of monomers used and the conditions under which they are synthesised. For instance, low density (LD) and high density (HD) poly(ethene) are derived from ethene. Thermosoftening polymers melt upon heating, whereas thermosetting polymers remain solid when heated.

RAPPING UP!

Alloys are useful **materials**.
In rims or the core of the steer wheel.
Make them by melting different metals
then mix them up like **milk and cereal**.

What you get now has two properties.
And it can do a task more properly.
We use them every day in life.
For example, here some **commodities**.

Bronze, brass, steel, **nichrome**,
even titanium up in this iPhone.
Gold needs zinc to make it ideal
and for knives we use stainless steel.

Mixed together they're harder.
You might be wondering why.
It's 'coz some **atoms** are larger
as a result the layers can't slide.

Thermosoftening plastics, including plastic bags, lack covalent bonds between their chains. Consequently, they melt readily and can be recycled efficiently.

Thermosetting plastics, such as plugs, have covalent bonds between their chains. This property means they do not melt easily, making them suitable for electrical appliances that can become hot.

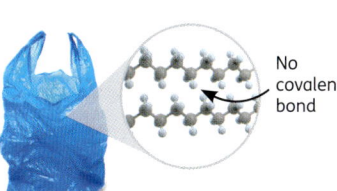 No covalent bond

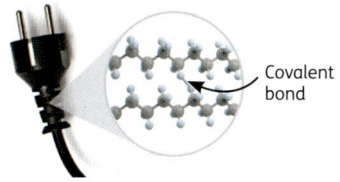 Covalent bond

The Haber Process

Ammonia (NH_3) is a compound used in the manufacture of fertilisers, plastics and dyes. It consists of nitrogen and hydrogen elements. The reaction is reversible:

$$N_{2(g)} + 3H_{2(g)} \rightleftharpoons 2NH_{3(g)}$$

Key facts

- Ammonia is produced using the Haber process and is important in the production of fertilisers.
- The Haber process uses nitrogen from the air and hydrogen from methane.
- The Haber process works best at low temperatures and high pressures, with optimal conditions being 200 atmospheres pressure, 450°C (842°F), and the use of a catalyst.

Due to nitrogen being an unreactive gas, creating ammonia necessitates a catalyst. The Haber process uses iron as a catalyst to facilitate the reaction between nitrogen and hydrogen gases to produce liquid ammonia.

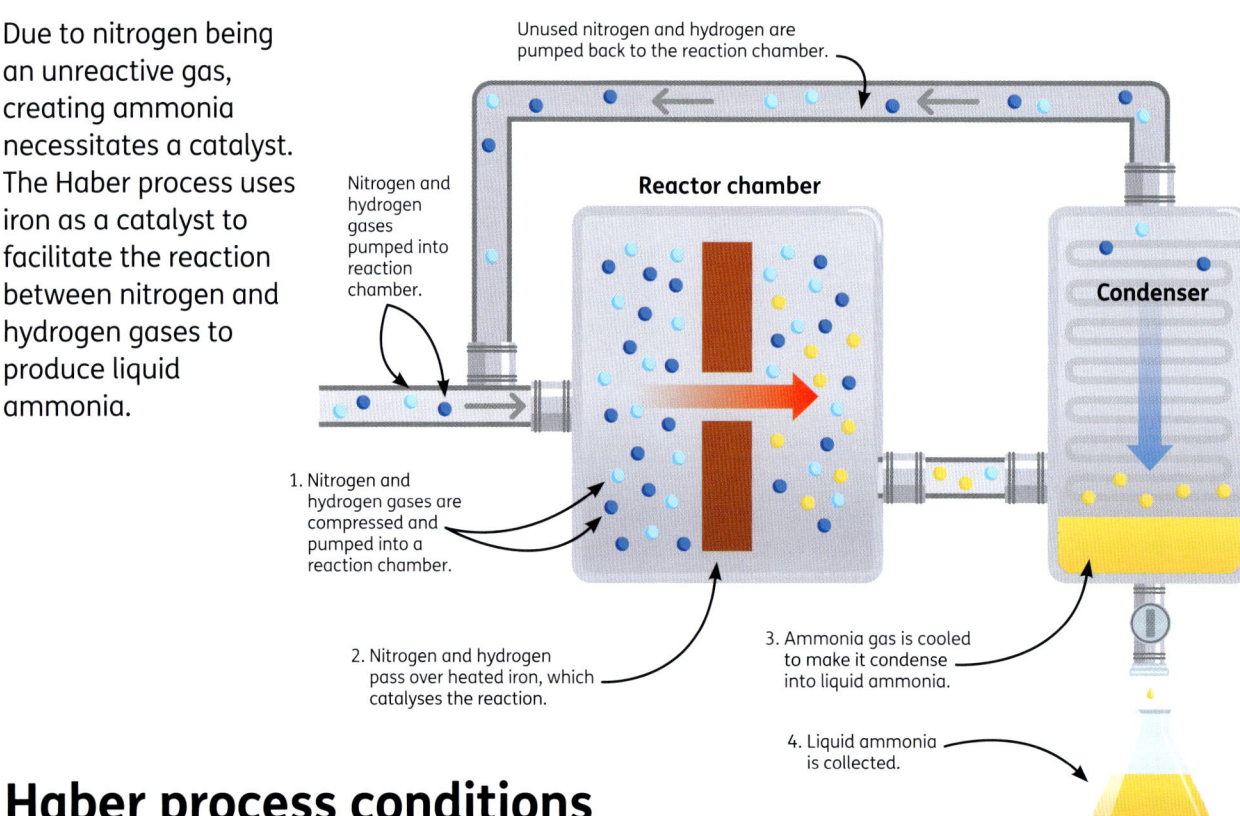

1. Nitrogen and hydrogen gases are compressed and pumped into a reaction chamber.
2. Nitrogen and hydrogen pass over heated iron, which catalyses the reaction.
3. Ammonia gas is cooled to make it condense into liquid ammonia.
4. Liquid ammonia is collected.

Unused nitrogen and hydrogen are pumped back to the reaction chamber.

Haber process conditions

The chemical industry aims to maximise product yield by producing as much product as quickly as possible. The Haber process is a reversible reaction that is slow and produces a limited amount of ammonia. Scientists can improve this efficiency by altering the reaction conditions. The optimum conditions for the Haber process are 200 atmospheres pressure, 450°C, and with the use of an iron catalyst. The conditions chosen are a compromise between speed, yield and cost.

Pressure	Increasing the pressure increases the yield but is expensive and dangerous.	Decreasing the pressure reduces the yield.
Temperature	Increasing the temperature decreases the yield, but increases the rate of reaction.	Decreasing the temperature increases the yield, but the reaction proceeds very slowly.

Fertilisers

Plants absorb specific elements from the soil necessary for their growth. As these elements are depleted over time, farmers and gardeners must replenish them by applying fertilisers. These chemical substances contain soluble compounds that provide the essential elements required by plants.

Key facts

- Plants need elements from the soil to grow: mainly nitrogen (N), phosphorus (P) and potassium (K).
- Fertilisers must be soluble and provide these essential elements.
- Fertilisers are produced either in laboratories or industrially.

NPK fertilisers

Artificial fertilisers, known as NPK fertilisers, contain varying ratios of nitrogen, N (aids growth), phosphorus, P (helps with both photosynthesis and respiration), and potassium, K (helps with opening and closing stomata in plant leaves). Plants absorb these elements as soluble compounds.

Fertiliser production

Fertilisers can be produced in a laboratory using simple equipment. The heat generated by the reaction is used to evaporate water from the fertiliser, increasing its concentration. Producing fertilisers in a laboratory is done on a much smaller scale than in industrial settings.

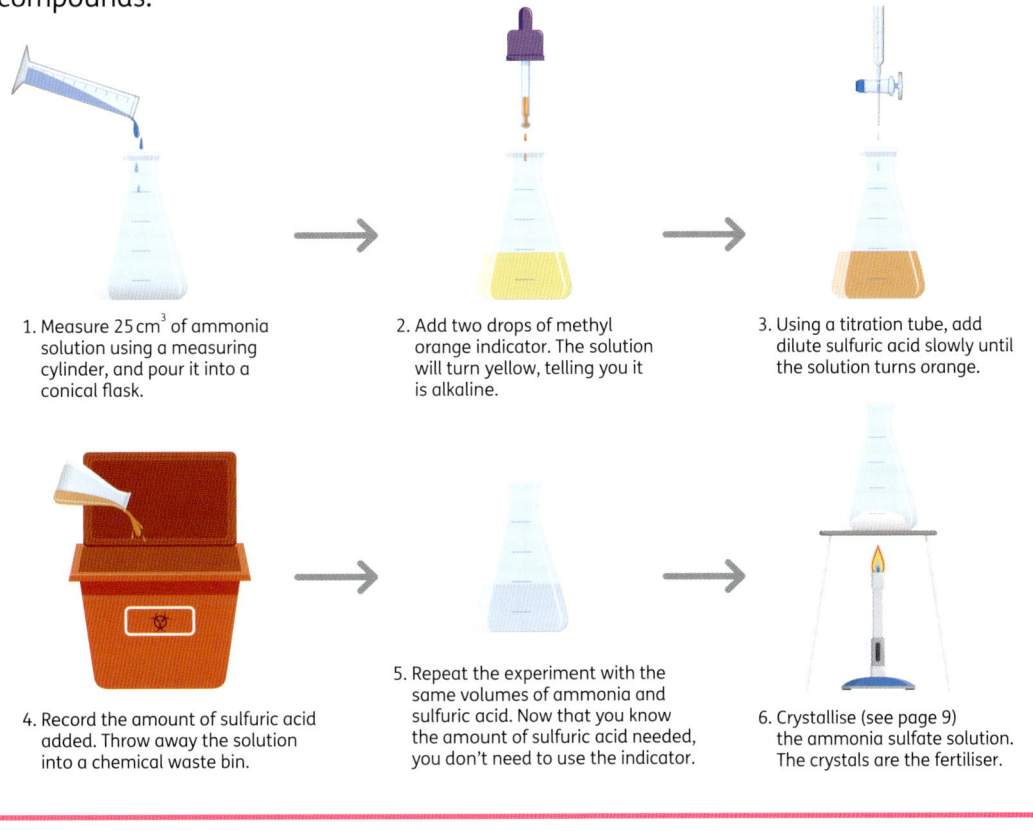

1. Measure 25 cm³ of ammonia solution using a measuring cylinder, and pour it into a conical flask.
2. Add two drops of methyl orange indicator. The solution will turn yellow, telling you it is alkaline.
3. Using a titration tube, add dilute sulfuric acid slowly until the solution turns orange.
4. Record the amount of sulfuric acid added. Throw away the solution into a chemical waste bin.
5. Repeat the experiment with the same volumes of ammonia and sulfuric acid. Now that you know the amount of sulfuric acid needed, you don't need to use the indicator.
6. Crystallise (see page 9) the ammonia sulfate solution. The crystals are the fertiliser.

ammonia + sulfuric acid ⟶ ammonium sulfate

$$2NH_{3(aq)} + H_2SO_{4(aq)} \longrightarrow (NH_4)_2SO_{4(aq)}$$

Brain Booster

Earth's Resources Recap Quiz

 Find a pen and paper and work through these revision questions.

1. State a definition for potable water.
2. What is sustainable development?
3. Explain the stages in waste water treatment.
4. What is phytomining?
5. What is bioleaching?
6. What are ceramics and how are they made?
7. What is the difference between thermosoftening and thermosetting polymers?
8. What is a life cycle assessment (LCA)? Name the main stages of an LCA.
9. What is corrosion? Name **three** methods to prevent corrosion.
10. What are alloys? Give **two** examples of commonly used alloys.
11. What is the Haber process?
12. How is the Haber process significant for agriculture?
13. Why are fertilisers important for plant growth?

Check your answers on page 110.

Answers

Atomic Structure and the Periodic Table 14

1. The number of protons in the nucleus of an atom.
2. Protons (positive charge), neutrons (no charge), and electrons (negative charge).
3. A nucleus containing protons and neutrons, surrounded by electrons in electron shells.
4. A diagram with 2 electrons in the inner shell, 8 electrons in the next shell and 1 electron in the outer shell.
5. Formed when atoms lose or gain electrons to achieve a full outer electron shell.
6. In order of increasing atomic number, in groups with similar properties.
7. They have full outer electron shells, achieving a stable electron configuration.
8. Using filtration.
9. Phosphorus has 5 electrons in its outer shell.
10. Metals: typically shiny, good conductors of heat and electricity, malleable and ductile. Non-metals: often dull, poor conductors of heat and electricity, and brittle.
11. They emit bright colours when an electric current passes through them.
12. 6 neutrons. Carbon's atomic number is 6 and its mass number is 12. 12 − 6 = 6.
13. They have the same number of outer electrons.

Bonding, Structure and Properties of Matter 24

1. Bond formed when atoms transfer electrons from one to another, resulting in positive and negative ions. The electrostatic attraction between these oppositely charged ions is known as an ionic bond.
2. Some common examples: water (H2O), carbon dioxide (CO2), methane (CH4), hydrogen chloride (HCl) and ammonia (NH3).
3. High melting and boiling points and conduct electricity when molten or dissolved in water.
4. C_{60}
5. A shared pair of electrons between two atoms.
6. It has delocalised electrons that can move freely between layers, allowing it to conduct electricity.
7. They have weak intermolecular forces, which require less energy to overcome.
8. There is a transfer of electrons from sodium to chlorine, which means that it is ionic bonding.
9. The substance is likely to have ionic bonding.
10. In water because the ions are free to move, whereas in solid form the ions are fixed in place.
11. Copper conducts electricity due to free electrons, while diamond does not conduct electricity because it has no free electrons.
12. Graphene is highly conductive, strong and flexible, making it ideal for electronic devices. However, manufacturing challenges and cost are significant considerations.

Quantitative Chemistry 32

1. 18 (2 for H + 16 for O)
2. 2 moles (88 g ÷ 44)
3. 116 g (2 × 23 for Na + 35.5 for Cl)
4. The total mass of reactants equals the total mass of products.
5. 25 g (mass of reactants = mass of products)
6. 80% (20 ÷ 25 × 100)
7. 45 g (50 ÷ 100 × 90)
8. A measure of the efficiency of a reaction in terms of how well atoms in reactants are utilised in the products. It is important for reducing waste and improving sustainability.
9. 100% (mass of desired product ÷ mass of all reactants) × 100
10. By taking the relative atomic masses of the constituent atoms from the periodic table and then finding the sum.
11. 50 g (0.5 × 100)
12. 12 moles (144 g ÷ 12)
13. 294 g (3 × 98 g/mol)

Chemical Changes 42

1. metal + acid → salt + hydrogen
2. Metals in order of reactivity with the most reactive metals at the top and the least reactive at the bottom.
3. Sodium ions move to the cathode and are reduced to sodium metal, while chloride ions migrate to the anode and are oxidised to chlorine gas.
4. Cathode product: hydrogen Anode product: chlorine
5. Strong acids ionise completely in water. Weak acids only partially ionise.
6. The pH range for acidic solutions is 0 to 6.
7. A known volume of an acid or a base is slowly added to a known volume of another acid or base until the reaction reaches an end-point, indicated by a colour change of an indicator.
8. Produced by reacting an acid with an insoluble base.
9. Sodium ions (Na^+), hydrogen ions (H^+), hydroxide ions (OH^-) and chloride ions (Cl^-)
10. Hydrochloric acid (HCl), sulfuric acid (H_2SO_4), and nitric acid (HNO_3)
11. They form a metal oxide.
12. The process in which a substance loses electrons or gains oxygen.

Energy Changes 50

1. A chemical reaction that releases energy in the form of heat.
2. Combustion of fuels, respiration and neutralisation reactions
3. An endothermic reaction absorbs energy from its surroundings.
4. It shows the energy of reactants higher than the energy of products.
5. It shows the energy of reactants lower than the energy of products.
6. The bond energy is the amount of energy required to break one mole of a bond in a gaseous state. By finding the sum of the bond energies of all the bonds broken in the reactants and subtracting the bond energies of all bonds formed in the products, the overall bond energy change for the reaction can be calculated.
7. Hydrogen fuel cells generate electricity through a chemical reaction between hydrogen and oxygen. Hydrogen molecules at the anode are split into protons and electrons, with the protons passing through an electrolyte and the electrons creating an electric current. At the cathode, protons, electrons and oxygen combine to form water, the only by-product.
8. A device that generates electrical energy from chemical reactions through the transfer of electrons.
9. copper–magnesium
10. Fuel cells are generally more efficient due to direct energy conversion.
11. Reactants: total bond energy of the reactants:
    H–H bond energy: 436 kJ/mol
    Br–Br bond energy: 193 kJ/mol
    Total bond energy of reactants = 436 + 193 = 629 kJ/mol
    Products: total bond energy of the products:
    2 H–Br bond energies: 2 × 366 = 732 kJ/mol
    Bond energy change = total bond energy of reactants − total bond energy of products
    Bond energy change = 629 kJ/mol − 732 kJ/mol = −103 kJ/mol
12. Compare the recharging methods and efficiency levels of both rechargeable devices and continuous operation fuel systems. Rechargeable devices rely on electrical input, while continuous operation systems utilise fuel, providing uninterrupted energy. From an efficiency standpoint, rechargeable systems often face energy conversion losses, making them generally less efficient. In contrast, fuel systems achieve higher efficiency through direct energy conversion. Applications of these systems also vary: rechargeable systems are commonly found in portable devices and electric vehicles, whereas fuel systems are preferred in scenarios demanding high efficiency and clean energy, such as spacecraft and certain vehicles.

Rates of Reaction 58

1. The speed at which reactants are converted to products.
2. Monitoring the change in concentration of reactants/products over time and measuring the volume of gas produced in gas-forming reactions.

110 Answers

3. Collision theory states that, for a reaction to occur, reactant particles must collide with sufficient energy and proper orientation.
4. Increasing temperature increases the rate of a chemical reactant particles have more kinetic energy, leading to more frequent and energetic collisions.
5. Higher concentration of reactants increases the rate of reaction as it leads to more frequent collisions between reactant particles.
6. Larger surface area of reactants increases the rate of reaction by providing more area for collisions to occur.
7. A catalyst increases the rate of a reaction by lowering the activation energy required for the reaction to proceed, allowing more collisions to result in a reaction.
8. A reversible reaction is one where the reactants can form products, which can react to form the original reactants again.
9. When hydrated copper sulfate is heated, it loses water molecules and transforms into anhydrous copper sulfate ($CuSO_4$), which appears as a white powder. If water is added to anhydrous copper sulfate, the reverse reaction occurs, and hydrated copper sulfate is reformed, turning the substance back to its blue colour.
10. The symbol used to represent a reversible reaction is a double arrow ($\rightleftharpoons$).
11. Dynamic equilibrium occurs in reversible reactions when the rate of the forward reaction equals the rate of the reverse reaction, resulting in constant concentrations of reactant and product.
12. The minimum energy required for reactant particles to collide and form products according to collision theory.

Organic Chemistry 74

1. A fossil fuel formed over millions of years from the remains of ancient marine organisms. It is a mixture of hydrocarbons.
2. Alkanes are saturated hydrocarbons with single bonds between carbon atoms. The simplest alkane is methane (CH_4).
3. Alkenes are unsaturated hydrocarbons with at least one double bond between carbon atoms. General formula: C_nH_{2n}.
4. A process that separates crude oil into fractions based on boiling points by heating it and condensing the vapours.
5. A chemical process that breaks down large hydrocarbons into smaller, more useful ones, often using heat and catalysts.
6. Organic compounds with one or more hydroxyl (–OH) group attached to a carbon atom. Example: ethanol (C_2H_5OH).
7. Organic acids containing a carboxyl (–COOH) group. Example: acetic acid (CH_3COOH).
8. Formed from the reaction between an alcohol and a carboxylic acid, producing water. Example reaction: ethanol + acetic acid → ethyl acetate + water.
9. The joining of monomers with the loss of small molecules like water. It differs from addition polymerisation because it involves at least two types of monomer.
10. A molecule that carries genetic information in living organisms. It has a double helix structure composed of nucleotides.
11. Organic compounds that serve as the building blocks of proteins. General structure includes an amino (–NH_2) group and a carboxyl (–COOH) group.
12. Used in food flavourings, perfumes and as solvents in the chemical industry.

Chemical Analysis 84

1. A substance that consists of only one type of particle; there are no impurities or mixtures.
2. A pure substance has a specific and fixed melting point or boiling point. Impurities will cause these points to change.
3. A mixture that has been designed as a useful product. Each component in the mixture is present in a specific quantity.
4. Medications, paint, baby milk formula and cleaning products.
5. Insert a glowing splint into the gas. If the splint relights, oxygen is present.
6. Pass the gas through limewater. If the limewater turns cloudy, carbon dioxide is present.
7. Chlorine gas turns damp blue litmus paper red and then bleaches it white.
8. Ammonia gas has a pungent smell and turns damp red litmus paper blue.
9. Bring a lit splint near the gas. If a squeaky pop sound is heard, hydrogen is present.
10. Sodium ions produce a bright yellow flame in a flame test.
11. They react with sodium hydroxide to form a white precipitate that dissolves in excess sodium hydroxide.
12. They form a green precipitate when reacted with sodium hydroxide.
13. Add dilute acid to the substance. If carbon dioxide gas is produced, carbonate ions are present.
14. Add dilute nitric acid followed by silver nitrate. Chloride ions produce a white precipitate, bromide ions produce a cream precipitate, and iodide ions produce a yellow precipitate.
15. It offers higher sensitivity and specificity, and results can be obtained more quickly compared to traditional methods.
16. A technique used to analyse the wavelengths of light emitted by a sample when it is heated in a flame.

Chemistry of the Atmosphere 92

1. Nitrogen (78 per cent), oxygen (21 per cent), argon (0.9 per cent), and trace gases including carbon dioxide (0.04 per cent).
2. It released gases like water vapour, carbon dioxide, methane, ammonia and nitrogen, contributing to the formation of the early atmosphere.
3. Oxygen increased due to photosynthesis by algae and plants, converting carbon dioxide and water into oxygen and glucose.
4. Carbon dioxide decreased through processes such as photosynthesis and the formation of carbonate rocks in the oceans.
5. Carbon dioxide, methane, nitrous oxide and water vapour.
6. Heat is trapped in Earth's atmosphere, leading to warmer global temperatures.
7. Rising global temperatures, melting ice caps and increased frequency of extreme weather events.
8. It measures the total greenhouse gas emissions caused directly or indirectly by an individual, organisation, event or product.
9. It forms from incomplete combustion of fossil fuels, and affects human health by reducing oxygen delivery to organs and tissues.
10. It is caused by particulates in the atmosphere that block sunlight, leading to cooler surface temperatures.
11. It forms when sulfur dioxide and nitrogen oxides react with water vapour in the atmosphere to produce sulfuric and nitric acids, which fall as precipitation.
12. It contributes to smog and acid rain and can irritate the respiratory system.

Earth's Resources 108

1. Water that is safe to drink/fit for human consumption.
2. Development that meets the needs of the present without compromising the ability of future generations to meet their own needs.
3. Screening or filtering, biological treatment, aeration, and chemical treatment.
4. The process of extracting metals from soil using plants.
5. The extraction of metals from ores using bacteria.
6. Ceramics are non-metallic, inorganic materials made by heating clay or other materials at high temperatures.
7. Thermosoftening polymers can be melted and reshaped multiple times, Thermosetting polymers harden permanently after being shaped once.
8. The analysis of the environmental impact of a product throughout its entire life cycle. The main stages include extraction or mining, manufacturing or processing, use, disposal, and transport between each stage.
9. The deterioration of metals due to chemical reactions with the environment. Methods include coating, greasing, oiling, electroplating and galvanizing.
10. Materials made by combining two or more metals, or a metal with a non-metal. Examples: steel (iron and carbon), bronze (copper and tin), brass (copper and zinc).
11. A chemical reaction used to synthesise ammonia from nitrogen and hydrogen.
12. It provides a large-scale method to produce ammonia, essential for modern agriculture.
13. Fertilisers provide essential nutrients to plants, promoting growth and increasing crop yields.

Exam Board References

Pages	AQA	Edexcel
6–7	4.1.1.1, 4.1.1.4, 4.1.1.5, 4.1.1.6, 4.1.1.7	1.1–1.12, 1.19, 1.20
8–9	4.1.1.2	2.5–2.8
10–11	4.1.2.1, 4.1.2.2, 4.1.2.3	1.7–1.12, 1.13–1.18
12–13	4.1.2.4, 4.1.2.5, 4.1.2.6, 4.1.3, 4.1.3.1, 4.1.3.2	6.1–6.7
16–17	4.2.1.1, 4.2.1.2, 4.2.1.3, 4.2.2.3	1.21–1.27, 1.32–1.33
18–19	4.2.1.4, 4.2.2.4, 4.2.2.5	1.28–1.31, 1.34
20–21	4.2.2.6, 4.2.3.1, 4.2.3.2, 4.2.3.3	1.35–1.37, 1.39
22–23	4.2.1.5, 4.2.2.7, 4.2.2.8	1.40–1.42
26–27	4.1.1.1, 4.2.2.2, 4.3.1.1, 4.3.1.2, 4.3.1.3, 4.3.1.4	1.44–1.46, 1.49
28–29	4.3.2.1, 4.3.2.2, 4.3.2.3, 4.3.2.4, 4.3.2.5	–
30–31	4.3.3.1, 4.3.3.2, 4.3.4, 4.3.5	–
34–35	4.4.1.1, 4.4.1.2, 4.4.1.3, 4.4.1.4	3.1–3.5
36–37	4.4.2.1, 4.4.2.2, 4.4.2.3, 4.4.2.4, 4.4.2.6	3.5–3.10
38–39	4.4.2.5	–
44–45	4.5.1.1	7.10–7.13
46–47	4.5.1.2, 4.5.1.3	7.14–7.16
48–49	4.5.2.1, 4.5.2.2	5.25–5.27
52–53	4.6.1.1, 4.6.1.2	7.1–7.5
54–55	4.6.1.3, 4.6.1.4	7.6–7.8
56–57	4.6.2.1, 4.6.2.2, 4.6.2.3, 4.6.2.4, 4.6.2.5, 4.6.2.6, 4.6.2.7	4.13–4.17
60–61	4.7.1.1, 4.7.1.3	8.1–8.5
62–63	4.7.1.2	8.1–8.5
64–65	4.7.1.4	–
66–67	4.7.2.1, 4.7.2.2, 4.7.2.3	9.10–9.14
68–69	4.7.2.4	9.26–9.30
70–71	4.7.3.1, 4.7.3.2	9.17–9.23
72–73	4.7.3.3, 4.7.3.4	9.24–9.25
76–77	4.8.1.1, 4.8.1.2, 4.8.1.3	2.9–2.11
78–79	4.8.2.1, 4.8.8.2, 4.8.8.3, 4.8.8.4	9.2–9.5
80–81	4.8.3.1, 4.8.3.2, 4.8.3.3, 4.8.3.4, 4.8.3.5	9.2
82–83	4.8.3.6, 4.8.3.7	9.8
86–87	4.9.1.1, 4.9.1.2, 4.9.1.3, 4.9.1.4	8.18–8.22
88–89	4.9.2.1, 4.9.2.2, 4.9.2.3, 4.9.2.4	8.24–8.26
90–91	4.9.3.1, 4.9.3.2	8.24–8.26
94–95	4.10.1.1, 4.10.1.2,	2.12
96–97	4.10.1.3	–
98–99	4.10.1.4	–
100–101	4.10.2.1	4.11
102–103	4.10.3.1	5.2–5.3
104–105	4.10.3.2, 4.10.3.3	–
106–107	4.10.4.1, 4.10.4.2	–

Acknowledgments

The publisher would like to thank the following for their kind permission to reproduce their photographs:

(Key: a-above; b-below/bottom; c-centre; f-far; l-left; r-right; t-top)

8 Science Photo Library: (br); GIPHOTOSTOCK (bl). **9 Science Photo Library:** GIPHOTOSTOCK (tl).
12 Dorling Kindersley: Ruth Jenkinson / RGB Research Limited (fbl, bl/Sodium, bl, bc, bc/Caesium, cb, crb, bc/Bromine, br).
13 Dorling Kindersley: Ruth Jenkinson / RGB Research Limited (cla, ca, cra, cl, c, cr).
Science Photo Library: Andrew Lambert Photography (b). **17 Science Photo Library:** Charles D. Winters (br).
20 Dreamstime.com: MinervaStudio (cr); Eduard Bonnin Turina (bc). Fotolia: apttone (cl).
22 Alamy Stock Photo: Yuen Man Cheung (br). **23 Dorling Kindersley:** Ruth Jenkinson / RGB Research Limited (tl).
26 Dorling Kindersley: Ruth Jenkinson / Holts Gems (cb). **28 Science Photo Library:** (cb).
31 Science Photo Library: Andrew Lambert Photography (tc, tr); Science Source (bl, bc, br).
36 Science Photo Library: Martyn F. Chillmaid (b). **37 123RF.com:** imagepixels (tr); maksym yemelyanov / maxxyustas (ftl); mrtwister (tc/rain). **Dreamstime.com:** Denira777 (tl); Puripat Khummungkhoon (tc); Winnipuhin (ftr).
39 Science Photo Library: Charles D. Winters (bl). **44 123RF.com:** Romolo Tavani (cra).
45 Science Photo Library: GIPHOTOSTOCK (tr). **48 Dreamstime.com:** Yudesign (cr). **49 Science Photo Library:** Mikkel Juul Jensen (c). **52 123RF.com:** Romolo Tavani (cr). **Science Photo Library:** GIPHOTOSTOCK (c); Paul Rapson (cl).
53 Alamy Stock Photo: sciencephotos (b). **Science Photo Library:** Trevor Clifford Photography (cr).
56 Science Photo Library: Martyn F. Chillmaid (bl, bc). **57 Science Photo Library:** Turtle Rock Scientific / Science Source (bl). **60 Science Photo Library:** Crown Copyright / Health & Safety Laboratory (br).
63 123RF.com: Scanrail (ca). **Alamy Stock Photo:** Nathan Allred (ca/petrol). **Dreamstime.com:** Ilfede (cb). PunchStock: Westend61 / Rainer Dittrich (c). **Science Photo Library:** Victor De Schwanberg (bc); Paul Rapson (tr, c/Naphtha).
76 Alamy Stock Photo: Evgeny Karandaev (cb). **Science Photo Library:** Martyn F. Chillmaid (cr). **Shutterstock.com:** Krasula (bl). **77 Getty Images / iStock:** E+ / Mitshu (cr). **79 Science Photo Library:** Martyn F. Chillmaid (c).
80 Science Photo Library: (bl). **81 Science Photo Library:** (bc, bc/bromides, br); GIPHOTOSTOCK (t). **96 Alamy Stock Photo:** Robert Brook / Science Photo Library (cb). **Dreamstime.com:** Win Nondakowit (c). **Science Photo Library:** Robert Brook (bc).
99 Dreamstime.com: Cloki (br); Subodh Sathe (cr).
101 123RF.com: Aleksey Poprugin (bl). **102 123RF.com:** Nik Merkulov (clb). **104 Dreamstime.com:** Yifang Zhao (c).
105 123RF.com: Aleksey Poprugin (bc). **Dreamstime.com:** Ib Photography / Inbj (br/plug)

Cover images: Front and Back: **Adobe Stock:** miloje (Textured Background); Back: **Dreamstime.com:** Beaniebeagle clb/ (Tubes), Vladimir Gladcov clb, Sergey Kolesov clb/ (Mark), Mex D clb/ (brain), Ylivdesign clb/ (explosion)

About the author

Matt Green, aka The Rapping Science Teacher, is a TikTok sensation, TV broadcaster, author and business owner, famous for his viral rapping science videos across social media.

Thanks to Matt's educational and entertaining videos and his performances of acclaimed freestyles on TV and radio, Matt, the former Head of Chemistry at a London comprehensive school, now has millions of followers across his social media platforms and is a regular guest on primetime TV and radio shows.

Content creator Matt works with many leading brands, and uses his teaching skills to educate and entertain students on social media by releasing 30-second GCSE science rap videos every week, with subjects ranging from respiration to electrolysis, teamed with chart-topping soundtracks.

Matt now brings you three new revision guides with his famous TikTok raps to help you to **Rap. Revise. Remember!**